LOYAL DISSENTERS

*Reading Scripture and Talking Freedom
with 17th-century English Baptists*

LEE CANIPE

Also by Lee Canipe

*A Baptist Democracy:
Separating God from Caesar in the Land of the Free*

Advance Praise for *Loyal Dissenters*

Lee Canipe's wonderful book *Loyal Dissenters* is a must-read for all who care about Baptist history and current religious-liberty debates. He makes a powerful case that we freedom-loving Baptists trace our roots to 17th-century religious dissenters, not the 18th-century Enlightenment; to injunctions found in Scripture, more than philosophical reasoning. At the same time, our forebears' dissent co-existed with loyalty to Caesar, as far as that allegiance did not run headlong into the fear of God. At our best, we Baptists (more than, say, our Anabaptist cousins) continue to be both/and people: free children of God and good citizens, too.

—*J. Brent Walker*
Executive Director, Baptist Joint Committee for Religious Liberty

Lee Canipe writes as a "scholar-pastor," a tradition that extends back to the Reformation in Protestantism and all the way to the second century in the broader Christian tradition. In short, he brings the insights of scholarly training to the pastoral task of guiding us on how to think (and act) about religious liberty. This book is a reminder that early Baptists neither had nor needed the Enlightenment to show them how to think about religious liberty. They took their arguments from the ancient and authoritative text of their faith—the Bible.

—*Barry Hankins*
Professor of History, Baylor University

At a time when the question of religious liberty is, sadly, again a matter of pressing concern, Lee Canipe's challenging study is a most welcome addition to an increasingly important issue both for Christians and the international community. He examines the theological and historical roots of the earliest Baptists' advocacy of universal freedom of religion and opposition to religious persecution, arguing that their basis does not lie in abstract human rights, but in God's revealed word in Scripture. Through telling their story, examining their writings, and his own sermons based on texts used by them, the author provides us with a readable, by no means superficial, and provocative study which will benefit those new to this vital discussion, as well as those who want to develop their thinking on this most vital of subjects.

—*Anthony R. Cross*
Department of Theology and Religion, Oxford University

Smyth & Helwys Publishing, Inc.
6316 Peake Road
Macon, Georgia 31210-3960
1-800-747-3016
©2016 by Lee Canipe
All rights reserved.

Library of Congress Cataloging-in-Publication Data

Names: Canipe, Lee, 1970- author.
Title: Loyal dissenters : reading scripture and talking freedom with
17th-century English Baptists / by Lee Canipe.
Description: Macon : Smyth & Helwys, 2016. | Includes bibliographical
references.
Identifiers: LCCN 2016010444 | ISBN 9781573128728 (pbk. : alk. paper)
Subjects: LCSH: Baptists--England--History--17th century. |
Baptists--Doctrines--History--17th century. | England--Church
history--17th century.
Classification: LCC BX6276 .C28 2016 | DDC 286.0942/09032--dc23
LC record available at http://lccn.loc.gov/2016010444

Disclaimer of Liability: With respect to statements of opinion or fact available in this work of nonfiction, Smyth & Helwys Publishing Inc. nor any of its employees, makes any warranty, express or implied, or assumes any legal liability or responsibility for the accuracy or completeness of any information disclosed, or represents that its use would not infringe privately-owned rights.

*Dedicated to the glory of God
and
the community of believers at
Murfreesboro Baptist Church*

Contents

Acknowledgments   ix

Introduction   1

Chapter 1
Tumultuous Times
17th-century English Baptists in Context   17

Chapter 2
Reading Scripture with 17th-century English Baptists
A Brief Primer   39

Chapter 3
Conviction
Civil Authority Has No Power over Religion   53

Chapter 4
Conviction
Persecution on Account of Religion Is Wrong   79

Chapter 5
Conviction
Loyalty to the King, Obedience to God   111

Conclusion
Getting It Right
Faith, Freedom, and a Distinctive Baptist Witness   143

Bibliography   153

Acknowledgments

I've learned that any project worth doing will, at some point—and out of necessity—become a team effort. The poet John Donne wrote that "No man is an island," and I, for one, am glad of it. Otherwise, this book may never have gotten started. It certainly would not have been completed. Many individuals, and a few institutions, helped me get this work done. I am profoundly grateful for their generous, cheerful assistance.

This book began to take shape in my imagination well over a decade ago while I was still a graduate student at Baylor. It didn't actually start to materialize, however, until fall 2009, when Murfreesboro Baptist Church, where I serve as pastor, gave me the generous gift of a lengthy study leave. Thanks to an invitation from the Graduate Theological Foundation to study at Oxford University through the foundation's Oxford Fellows Program, I had the opportunity to spend that leave time in England, where I was able to do almost all of the research for this book. The foundation fellowship gave me access to Oxford's Bodleian Library, which was a wonderful resource. More important, the fact that I was in Oxford allowed me to spend many hours at the Angus Library at Regent's Park College, which houses one of the largest and most comprehensive collections of Baptist historical documents in the world. Emma Walsh, the college librarian, granted me access to the archives and provided me with space to spread out and work. Library assistant Emily Burgoyne graciously answered every one of my requests with a friendly smile. I am also thankful to Anthony Cross, director of the Centre for

Baptist History and Heritage, for both his hospitality and his encouragement.

Despite all the assistance I received in Oxford, it still took a while for this project to come together—much longer, in fact, than I ever anticipated. Keith Gammons at Smyth & Helwys was extraordinarily patient with me, and I appreciate his confidence in my work. I also appreciate the people at Chowan University who offered me logistical support: Deborah Baugham, who handles interlibrary loan requests at Whitaker Library, and provost Danny Moore, who provided me with a small office on campus. Sage advice from Dean Lawson, a historian of early modern England, and Philip Thompson, who teaches theology at Sioux Falls Seminary in South Dakota, greatly improved the quality of this book. Both of these scholars read early drafts of chapters, and I welcomed their constructive criticism. Any stubborn errors of fact or interpretation that remain in this book are mine alone. I am especially indebted to Lou Ann Gilliam, the deacon chair at Murfreesboro Baptist Church this past year, for making it possible for me to take time away from my pastoral responsibilities and finally finish this book.

As always, my wife, Hilary, has been a constant source of encouragement, blessing, and joy. I couldn't do what I do without her. Our children—Helen, Watt, and Peter—make me proud every day to be their dad. They remind me that God is indeed good.

I had a lot of help getting this project completed. It truly would not have been possible, however, without the generous support of the people I serve at Murfreesboro Baptist Church. They gave me the time and the freedom to research, travel, and write. I am keenly aware that not every pastor is given such gifts. They also listened to the sermons in chapters 3, 4, and 5 of this book and offered their own opinions of what I had to say. I am both humbled and challenged by the trust that these Christians have invested in me. It is, then, with a great deal of gratitude and much joy that I dedicate this book to the glory of God and to the people I serve in the name of Jesus at Murfreesboro Baptist Church.

Lee Canipe
Murfreesboro, North Carolina

Introduction

Anti-Christian: Why come you not to church?
Christian: What should I do there?
Anti-Christian: Worship God.
Christian: I must worship God as He requireth and not as any mortal man requireth.
Anti-Christian: True, but the worship that we require you to offer up is the worship God requireth.
Christian: If it be so, I will with all willingness assent unto it. But my conscience must be satisfied thereof by the word of truth, that I may have faith in it, otherwise it is my grievous sin (Romans 14:22). For I may not believe it so to be because you affirm it.[1]

In volume 1 of Adam Taylor's *History of the English General Baptists*, there is a delightful story that may or may not be true. Either way, the story tells us something about the way that Taylor, writing in 1818, and his fellow Baptists understood their shared past as religious outsiders in a country that, relatively speaking, had only recently begun to tolerate religious outsiders. The story goes that, in 1691, Thomas Grantham, perhaps the best-known General Baptist pastor, author, and spokesman of the seventeenth century, returned to the eastern English town of Norwich to lead the church he had planted some years earlier. "His labours were great," Taylor wrote, "and his success encouraging: many were induced to give themselves up to the church and profess their faith in Christ by baptism."[2]

As fate would have it, Grantham's meeting house stood near St. Stephen's Church. The Anglican vicar at St. Stephen's, John Connauld, was "a worthy, pious, and learned clergyman, but sincerely attached to the doctrine and discipline of the established church."[3] In other words, Connauld represented a kinder, gentler version of the power structure that for years had relentlessly hounded Baptists such as Grantham for refusing to conform to the Church of England's standards of faith and religious practice. Conflict between the two ministers seemed inevitable, and their proximity to one another only heightened the tension—especially with Grantham regularly criticizing the Church of England from the pulpit and challenging his neighbor to public debates. It didn't help matters, of course, that Grantham's dynamic preaching had begun to attract members of the St. Stephen's Church to his little Baptist congregation.

Finally, an exasperated Connauld responded to Grantham's challenge on 17 April 1691 with a polite note requesting "a plain and positive answer to two questions of doctrine on church polity and baptism."[4] Grantham replied the same day. Thus began a remarkable correspondence that lasted for several months and generated more than sixty letters in all. While neither man ever changed his mind, this exchange of letters laid the foundation for a warm and unlikely friendship. Connauld frequently invited the Baptist to visit him at the parish house and offered him free use of his library. Grantham, meanwhile, often sought the advice of his Anglican colleague "in all cases of doubt or difficulty."[5] What began as a polite but pointed theological dispute became a surprisingly genuine friendship in which both parties agreed to disagree while holding each another in the highest regard. Such things simply did not happen between Baptists and Anglicans in seventeenth-century England.

But there's more. After a long and fruitful life, Grantham died on 17 January 1692. And who officiated at the funeral of this dyed-in-the-wool Baptist? None other than his Anglican friend, the Reverend Connauld, who declared at the service that, with the death of Thomas Grantham, "this day has a great man fallen in Israel."[6] Afraid that Grantham's enemies (and, after years of defying both the established church and the religious laws of England, Grantham did indeed have many enemies) would abuse the great man's corpse if his body was buried outdoors in a normal graveyard, Connauld insisted that Grantham be interred in the middle aisle of St. Stephen's Church. Eleven years later, Connauld died and, at his request, was buried beside his Baptist friend. Again, such things simply did not happen between Baptists and Anglicans in seventeenth-century England.

Of course, it may not have happened at all. Grantham historian Clint Bass, for one, has his doubts about the accuracy of Taylor's account, the main problems—and, admittedly, they're big ones—being that there is neither a middle aisle at St. Stephen's Church in Norwich nor any record of Grantham's burial there.[7] True or not, however, the fact that Taylor included this heartwarming tale in his history suggests that English Baptists in the early nineteenth century understood themselves to be the heirs of a movement that not only challenged the religious establishment of England while remaining committed to the nation's welfare but also—and more scandalous still—passionately believed that such a delicate balancing act was indeed possible. To put it another way, Baptists could be true to their consciences and still be good neighbors, their unconventional beliefs about baptism and church governance posing no threat to national security (as many people in seventeenth-century England feared) and their Christian convictions capable of winning the admiration—if not the approval—of those who were willing to engage them in conversation, respectable Anglican clergymen included. As portrayed in Adam Taylor's history, the early English Baptists were nothing less than loyal dissenters, willing to give the king his due, but not a bit more than that.

This book is about how these loyal dissenters marked the contested boundaries between what was, in fact, due to their earthly sovereign and what belonged exclusively to their Lord Jesus Christ. More specifically, it is about how their reading of Scripture drove them to three startling convictions—startling, at least, in the context of seventeenth-century England—that eventually came to define them as Christians of a distinctive sort. First, their reading of Scripture convinced them that civil powers have no legitimate authority over matters of faith. Second, their reading of Scripture convinced them that persecuting people for their religious beliefs was wrong. Third, their reading of Scripture convinced them that Christians must be obedient to the king's officials in all civil affairs but only to God in matters of religion. Binding these convictions together, of course, is the fact that Baptists in seventeenth-century England located them all in the written word of God. As "Christian" in John Murton's fictional dialogue insisted, only the "word of truth" could satisfy a Baptist's conscience. Nothing else would suffice. Simply put, when early English Baptists wanted to articulate what they believed about the proper relationship between God and king—and why they believed as they did—they unfailingly turned first to the Bible.

It's easy to forget this basic fact, primarily because Baptists in North America and Western Europe today live in societies where religious liberty—that is, a person's right to decide whether, what, and how to believe and practice his or her faith in God (or in anything else, for that matter) according to individual conscience and without interference from the government—can, for the most part, be happily taken for granted. In other words, they no longer have to make their arguments for religious liberty from scratch. Instead, Baptists in the United States can (and frequently do) point to the First Amendment to the Constitution prohibiting the establishment of religion and protecting its free exercise as the state's recognition of a self-evident truth. As the late James Dunn, a longtime advocate for religious liberty, frequently asserted, Baptists consider freedom of religion for all people to be an axiomatic conviction and a basic human right.[8] These are all happy developments, and Baptists in the United States and beyond should rightfully be proud of their historic commitment to what is now recognized—in the West, at least—as an inalienable human right.

Particular faith convictions that become general axioms, however, have a way of losing their distinctive character as *bona fide* faith convictions, especially if those who hold them forget where they came from and why they have them in the first place. Perhaps a personal anecdote can illustrate this point. When my wife and I lived in Texas, we passed on our way to church each Sunday a shop filled with either antiques or junk, depending on one's perspective. (The line between the two can indeed be exceedingly fine.) One morning as we passed by the shop, we saw a huge, rusty metal star leaning on the wall outside. We had been looking for something like this to fill a bare spot on one of our walls but had yet to discover the right decoration. The rusty star immediately struck us both as a promising, if unorthodox, candidate. So, after church, I returned to the shop, inquired about the star, and decided to make the purchase. As the shop owner totaled the bill, I wondered out loud what purpose the star might have once served. Was it a small, surviving relic from a bigger, long-lost something? My imagination wandered. Could it, for example, have once adorned an old bank building? A train? A ship? Did this star have a romantic past? Had it seen great adventure? I had to know.

So I asked, "What was this star?" The shop owner leaned forward, as if prepared to share a great but burdensome secret. "Well," he answered slowly and carefully, "it was used as a star." "I know *that*," I replied. "I'm just curious as to why someone would make a big metal star in the first place." The shop owner replied, once again, slowly and carefully. I realized now that his tone of voice wasn't so much conspiratorial as it was infinitely patient, the kind of voice one uses to explain complicated matters to small children. "If someone wanted a star," he said, "then I reckon they'd make a star." Convinced that further probing was futile, I paid for my star and headed for home, certain that I had in my possession a genuine, rusty metal star that may or may not have had a fascinating history but was, without a doubt, a star.

Now, as the shop owner would attest, just about anybody could have recognized my rusty metal star as a star. No further story or explanation was needed to make that point. It was, indeed, self-evidently a star. Did that particular star have a history that might have made it distinctive—something more than just a generic star? Maybe so. But, with that one specific story associated with that one specific star forgotten, if not altogether lost, the only thing left was, well, a star.

Herein lies the point. Religious liberty may be recognized by the United Nations as a fundamental human right. It may be guaranteed by the First Amendment to the Constitution of the United States and eloquently championed by such founding fathers as Thomas Jefferson and James Madison. It may be one of the natural rights or entitlements that John Locke and other Enlightenment philosophers considered essential to civil equality. It may be, as Dunn put it, "the freedom fire that burns in the belly of every Baptist" as a consequence of the fact that "volitional capacity is written into our being. We are programmed to be choosers. Our software requires it."[9] These descriptions of religious liberty may all be true. They certainly appear with great regularity in Baptist conversations on the subject. The problem is that none of them describe religious liberty in a way that is necessarily—and distinctively—Christian. It is as though Baptists in the twenty-first century have come to believe that it is sufficient to identify religious liberty as one of their defining faith convictions without bothering to consider what makes it a distinctively Christian faith conviction in the first place, and not just a self-evident truth available to any reasonable person of any (or no) religious faith. While Baptists may have broadened the grounds on which their arguments for freedom are built in order to widen their appeal, the example of the early English Baptists reminds us that distinctively Christian convictions must, by definition, be grounded in something that is distinctively Christian.

A century before Jefferson and Madison, and decades before Locke, Baptists in seventeenth-century England were talking openly, eloquently, and bravely about freedom of conscience and the evils of religious persecution—and they were doing so not by appealing to abstract notions about natural rights or human nature but, rather, to the life and teachings of Jesus Christ and his earliest followers as recorded in the New Testament. When the early Baptists wanted to talk about freedom, they first read their Bibles—or, to put it perhaps more accurately, when the early Baptists read their Bibles, they ended up talking about freedom. Their tracts and essays were crammed, stuffed, and packed to the point of bursting with Scripture references, so much so that all the citations and quotations shoehorned into the texts and tacked onto the margins can be quite distracting for a twenty-first-century reader. Yet it is precisely this abundance of biblical evidence, and the authors' obvious respect for biblical authority, that makes the work of these seventeenth-century English Baptists so distinctive. The arguments they made about freedom of conscience were ones that only Christians—in particular, Christians who took the Bible seriously—could have made in good faith. The biblical witness is not incidental to these arguments, mere sacred window dressing on an otherwise secular edifice. It is, instead, stubbornly fundamental to the ways in which early English Baptists understood religious freedom as an integral part of their Christian witness.

Scripture, in other words, served as the primary lens through which they saw, and made sense of, the world. Starting with the truth revealed in God's word, they considered their circumstances in light of that truth and then decided how to respond in the most faithful way possible. That response is what we might call a theological conviction. Early Baptist convictions about freedom *proceeded* from what they learned in Scripture about the nature of God and how God has chosen to redeem creation from sin. To do otherwise—to begin with a particular conviction and then seek to support it with a handful of Bible verses—is called "proof-texting," and it puts the proverbial cart before the horse. When our seventeenth-century Baptist ancestors expressed their own convictions about freedom in their own writings, they connected the theological dots in a very deliberate order. They began with Scripture and, from there, proceeded to form the faith convictions about freedom that defined their distinctive Christian witness. By allowing the early English Baptists to speak for themselves and make their own arguments for what they believe, we discover that their conversations almost always seem to start with the Bible.

The spiritual descendants of these Baptists have tended to obscure, or at least downplay, this direct link between Scripture and the historic Baptist commitment to freedom of conscience. As British historian John Coffey points out, modern scholars who write about the development of religious toleration—and, eventually, liberty— in the Western world "sometimes bypass the specifically theological case for toleration in favor of concentrating on general philosophical arguments that could still be used in secular discussion today." Simply put, this is bad history. It is, Coffey writes, as if proponents of toleration "are abstracted from their context within 17th century Protestantism and forced to argue for toleration without any of the uniquely Christian arguments which were most calculated to influence their devout readers."[10] As New Testament scholar Luke Timothy Johnson has pointed out, the most obvious reason for this tendency is that the "Christian scriptures do not in any direct or obvious way provide support for the contemporary proposition that it is a human right to be religious."[11] J. D. Hughey, a student of church history and one-time president of the International Baptist Theological Seminary in Rüschlikon, Switzerland, recognized this quandary several decades ago. "Religious liberty is not a truth explicitly revealed in Scripture," he wrote in 1963, but it is nevertheless "implicit in Christian teaching." Accordingly, Hughey's argument for religious liberty relied not on specific biblical texts for support but, rather, on the practical implications of Jesus' love ethic, the Golden Rule, and the doctrine that all humans are created in the image of God.[12]

Other Baptists have followed his example. Whether the early English Baptists "appealed to history, Scripture, or practical arguments," historian Leon McBeth wrote, "the underlying base was their view of the spiritual essence of Christianity. They understood true religion not in a creedal or organizational sense, but in a spiritual sense," completely removed from any form of human interference.[13] Baptists, McBeth claims, instinctively understood that the essence of the Christian faith demanded freedom for individual consciences. From this perspective, then, any corroborating evidence along these lines that early Baptists gleaned from history or Scripture or philosophy served only to bolster convictions they already held. Their convictions, in other words, *preceded* their engagement with specific passages of Scripture. Walter Shurden, another Baptist historian, echoes McBeth's assessment. Throughout Christian history, he writes, people have used the Bible to support both freedom and persecution. It's true that Baptists called for religious freedom in part "because of how they read the Bible. Like all people, Baptists went to the Bible with lenses that refracted the truth of God to them in a certain way," and certain New Testament texts pointed them in the direction of freedom.[14] Nevertheless, "rather than basing their commitment to religious liberty on specific texts" that can be misused and abused, Shurden maintains that "Baptists have been more inclined to build on biblical principles"—that is to say, more general theological conclusions about God, humanity, and the nature of faith that take the whole scope, and not just selected verses, of Scripture into consideration.[15]

It must be said, however, that these various rationales for focusing on general principles rather than specific texts—that is, the fact that both supporters and opponents of religious persecution have used Scripture to defend their respective positions—are not entirely persuasive. After all, Baptists have historically looked to the Bible for guidance on various issues and, in so doing, found themselves on opposite sides of the proverbial fence: slavery, for example, in the nineteenth century; civil rights in the twentieth century; or same-sex relationships in the twenty-first century. As people who believe that Christians are both free and obligated to read Scripture, Baptists can and will inevitably arrive at different interpretations of what they find there. That's just part of who we are. Not all of these interpretations, of course, are right. History has a way of clarifying these matters. The fact that specific texts can be misused and abused, however, is no reason to downplay their significance in favor of more abstract "biblical principles." For people who take the Bible seriously, the best response to a bad interpretation of Scripture will always be, well, a *better* interpretation of Scripture.

Of course, latter-day Baptists can afford to deal in general "biblical principles" when they talk about religious liberty because their English Baptist ancestors in the seventeenth century did the heavy lifting necessary to construct sound arguments for faith, freedom, and conscience based on their readings of particular (but, as Johnson and Hughey both observe, hardly explicit) verses of Scripture. This difficult and delicate work required insight, imagination, and biblical fluency—all potentially valuable resources for Baptists who seek to articulate what they believe in specifically Christian language. Yet, for whatever reason, the actual arguments from Scripture that early English Baptists themselves made are rarely, if ever, part of Baptist conversations about religious liberty. We do ourselves (and, in truth, our tradition of inspired biblical interpretation) a disservice when we concentrate only on the principled conclusions that early Baptists drew about freedom while downplaying, dismissing, or (worse yet) ignoring altogether the many examples of how they interacted with the Bible in order to arrive at those conclusions.

This process of interacting with—and then applying—God's word is precisely what distinguishes a faith conviction from a self-evident, axiomatic truth. Both may end up in the same place, but they take very different roads to get there. To put it in terms of my aforementioned experience with the antique dealer, a faith conviction is a star of a particular, peculiar sort that comes with a particular, peculiar story. Christians have a word for that kind of story: we call it a *witness*. Describing religious liberty as a faith conviction, then, is an essential skill for Baptists to acquire, for when it comes to this particular Baptist "distinctive," *what* we believe does not, in the end, necessarily make us distinctive in the Western world. There was a time, obviously, when it did. Not anymore. *What* we believe may no longer set us apart—but *why* we believe does. *Why* we believe in religious liberty is indeed our distinctive Baptist witness to the world, and it began, in good Baptist fashion, not with generalized "biblical principles" (true as they may be) but with the Bible itself. That is where our English Baptist ancestors grounded their convictions about freedom and conscience, and I am convinced that reading (and interpreting) Scripture with these loyal dissenters of the seventeenth century can help us learn to talk about such things in ways that only Christians are capable of. This book is, I hope, a step in that direction.

Here, then, is how we shall proceed. Chapter 1 provides context for our engagement with English Baptists from the 1600s. To be sure, some readers find history tedious and will be tempted to skip this chapter. Please resist that urge. The loyal Baptist dissenters of the seventeenth century did not live in a vacuum. They were shaped and influenced (as are we) by circumstances of place and time, and, if we are going to participate in a conversation with them, we need to do what we can to acquaint ourselves with the turbulent—and, for twenty-first-century readers, quite foreign—world in which they lived, wrote, worshiped, and read the Bible. Otherwise, we will find it difficult to appreciate the precarious position of these Baptists who claimed, in the same breath, to be both loyal subjects of the king and dissenters from the king's religion.

Chapter 2 provides a brief introduction to the art of reading Scripture across time and space. Needless to say, the world has changed since the seventeenth century. Ideas about how to craft and evaluate an argument—and, more fundamentally, where moral, intellectual, and religious authority all properly reside—that our English Baptist ancestors took for granted may now sound strange to us. One response to this strangeness would be to dismiss their views as hopelessly antiquated and, thus, irrelevant for our more enlightened times. Responsible readers, however, are willing to work harder in order to understand better, which requires some imagination. We cannot read Scripture *in the exact same way* as an English Baptist in the seventeenth century would have read Scripture, but we can take note of how their worldview differs from ours and how that difference might have influenced their interpretation of Scripture. In other words, we can recognize that, figuratively speaking, we all come to the Bible wearing the latest style of reading glasses. By the end of chapter 2, we will be better equipped to imagine what it would have been like to read the Bible through seventeenth-century lenses—a skill that will, in turn, enable us to read Scripture alongside our Baptist ancestors more sympathetically in the chapters that follow.

In chapters 3 through 5, we shall explore, in turn, three faith convictions about freedom of conscience that these loyal dissenters of the 1600s derived from their reading of Scripture: civil powers have no legitimate authority over matters of faith, persecution on account of religion is wrong, and Christians must be obedient to the king in all civil affairs but only to God in matters of religion. Of particular interest will be the way they argued for these convictions on the basis of Scripture. We shall, in other words, read their arguments as they made them: not by appealing to generalized biblical principles but, rather, by looking to the specific examples of Jesus and his apostles as recorded in the New Testament.

This is, after all, precisely how our Baptist ancestors understood their task. "I will, by God's assistance," wrote John Murton in 1615, "prove most evidently by the Scriptures that none ought nor can be compelled to worship God to acceptance by any worldly means whatsoever."[16] Murton had been a member of John Smyth's church in Amsterdam, followed Thomas Helwys back to England in 1612, and eventually succeeded Helwys as pastor of the first Baptist congregation in England. For Murton and his contemporaries, the Bible stood alone as the only legitimate authority that Baptists recognized in matters of faith and religious obligation. Accordingly, then, they insisted that the case for freedom of conscience would either be won or lost on the basis of what Scripture revealed to be true. "If our opponents have not anything from Scripture against us, then let them yield," declared Leonard Busher in 1614. Otherwise, he continued, let them go ahead and state their case because, as 2 Timothy 3:16-17 declares, "all Scripture is given by inspiration of God, and is profitable for doctrine, for reproof, for correction, for instruction in righteousness: that the man of God may be perfect, thoroughly furnished unto all good works."[17]

Chapters 3 through 5 all contain four distinct sections. Think of them as four stages of an extended conversation across the centuries with our English Baptist ancestors about what we believe and why, using the book we share in common, the Bible, as our starting point. In the first stage, we will listen as early Baptist writers present their various arguments for a distinctive faith conviction and the biblical evidence on which those arguments rest. In the second stage, we will evaluate the strengths and weaknesses of these nearly four-hundred-year-old arguments from Scripture. Are they shaky or sound? Can they stand up to critical scrutiny? Do they rely on proof-texts—that is, verses selectively taken out of context in order to buttress a given opinion—or do they preserve the integrity of the biblical passages in question? In the third stage, we will read a sermon—one prepared for and preached in a twenty-first-century Baptist church—from a biblical text cited by early English Baptist writers in their arguments for freedom of conscience. If Baptist proclaimers hope to talk about historic Baptist faith convictions in historically Baptist fashion, then they need to engage God's word—and not the First Amendment, the writings of Thomas Jefferson, or some other equally high-minded but secular oracle—as their primary source for inspiration. Chapters 3 through 5 each offer an example of how it can be done. Finally, in the fourth stage of our conversation, we will consider practical examples of how these traditional Baptist faith convictions remain as relevant today as they were four hundred years ago.

Next, a few words about spelling, grammar, and biblical translations. Spelling in seventeenth-century England was an imprecise science, with one word sometimes spelled several different ways within the same publication. As one author has wryly remarked, there are only six surviving signatures of William Shakespeare, whose life spanned the last years of the sixteenth century and the first years of the seventeenth, and in each one of these autographs, the playwright spelled his name differently.[18] Not only do the variable spelling practices of seventeenth-century English writers present a challenge for contemporary readers, but their grammar and syntax—that is, the way they put their sentences together—can also make for rough sledding. While there are strong arguments for preserving the original spellings, abbreviations, and so forth, there are stronger arguments for standardizing these sometimes idiosyncratic elements of the text for the sake of clarity, comprehension, and convenience. I have, then, taken the liberty to do just that when quoting from the original works of seventeenth-century English Baptists. Purists may protest, but I suspect that most readers will be grateful for these minor stylistic modifications. As for the biblical translations, we will use the Geneva Bible for all quotations from Scripture. First published in 1560, this Bible was favored by Baptists and other dissenting Christians in England over the King James Version that appeared in 1611 as the official Bible of the established Anglican Church. When our English Baptist ancestors quoted Scripture, they most likely quoted the verses as rendered in the Geneva Bible. Accordingly, we shall do the same.

And, lastly, a disclaimer: this book is not intended to be an exhaustive catalog of the Scripture references found in seventeenth-century

English Baptist literature, nor of the writings that Baptists produced during this period. The selected biblical texts highlighted in the following pages represent only a fraction of the verses cited in the various books, tracts, and sermons of Baptists agitating for freedom of conscience during the tumultuous 1600s. Likewise, these texts come from the work of a handful of English Baptist writers. In addition to Grantham, we will in due course meet James Blackmore, Leonard Busher, George Hammon, William Jeffrey, John Merton, Thomas Monck, John Reve, William Reynolds, Samuel Richardson, Francis Smith, Francis Stanley, Roger Williams, and Joseph Wright. Some of their work was done together as, for example, in joint petitions from prison. Some of them, meanwhile, wrote alone. They were not, of course, the only English Baptists writing during this period, but even as far back as the 1800s, their work was considered to be representative by historians.

What I present in this book, then, is but a handful of the biblical passages that appear most frequently in the arguments of these particular loyal dissenters. As such, the texts themselves might stand as a kind of unofficial canon for Baptists who want to talk biblically about God and Caesar. Indeed, when English Baptists in the seventeenth century wanted to argue for freedom of conscience, they typically turned to these verses of Scripture first. Perhaps, in time, their twenty-first-century spiritual descendants can learn to do so as well.

Now, with these words of introduction out of the way, let us turn to the task at hand.

Notes

1. John Murton, "Persecution for Religion Judged and Condemned," in E. B. Underhill, *Tracts of Liberty of Conscience and Persecution, 1614–1661* (London: J. Haddon, 1846) 103.

2. Adam Taylor, *The History of the English General Baptists*, vol. 1 (London: T. Bore, 1818) 308.

3. Ibid.

4. Ibid.

5. Ibid., 310.

6. Ibid., 315.

7. See Clint Bass, "Thomas Grantham and General Baptist Theology," D.Phil. diss., University of Oxford, 2008, p. 51, n. 119.

8. James Dunn, "The Baptist Vision of Religious Liberty," in *Proclaiming the Baptist Vision: Religious Liberty*, ed. Walter B. Shurden (Macon GA: Smyth and Helwys, 1997) 34.

9. Ibid., 34, 32.

10. John Coffey, *Persecution and Toleration in Protestant England, 1558–1689* (Harlow, England: Longman, 2000) 58.

11. Luke Timothy Johnson, "Religious Rights and Christian Texts," in *Religious Human Rights in Global Perspectives*, ed. John Witte, Jr., and Johan van der Vyver (Boston: M. Nijhoff, 1996) 66.

12. See J.D. Hughey, "The Theological Frame of Religious Liberty," *Christian Century* 80 (6 November 1963): 1365–68.

13. H. Leon McBeth, *English Baptist Literature on Religious Liberty to 1689* (New York: Arno Press, 1980) 279–80.

14. Walter B. Shurden, "How We Got That Way," in *Proclaiming the Baptist Vision: Religious Liberty*, ed. Walter B. Shurden (Macon GA: Smyth & Helwys, 1997) 21.

15. Walter Shurden, *The Baptist Identity: Four Fragile Freedoms* (Macon GA: Smyth & Helwys, 1993) 48–49. One of the overarching principles Shurden mentions is the biblical view of persons created in the image of God, expressed most nobly in Psalm 8 (Shurden, "How We Got That Way," 22). James Dunn, meanwhile, cites Genesis 1:26-27 in order to make much the same point about human dignity and individual moral responsibility (Dunn, "The Baptist Vision of Liberty," 32). The habit of relying on general principles to make the argument for religious freedom is not limited to Baptists of more moderate inclinations; Southern Baptists do it too. *First Freedom: The Baptist Perspective on Religious Liberty*, ed. Thomas White, Jason G. Duesing, and Malcolm B. Yarnell III (Nashville: B&H Publishing Group, 2007) is a good resource for understanding contemporary Southern Baptist perspectives on religious liberty. Essays of particular interest are Barrett Duke, "The Christian Doctrine of Religious Liberty," 7–29, and Thomas White, "The Defense of Religious Liberty by the Anabaptists and English Baptists," 49–65. Both Duke and White sprinkle their accounts of religious liberty with Scripture references but are more concerned with the general theological and ethical principles at stake than with the implications of specific biblical texts. Also of note is Paige Patterson, "Mutually Exclusive or Biblically Harmonious? Religious Liberty and Exclusivity of Salvation in Jesus Christ," 31–48, in which the author makes ample use of Scripture in constructing his arguments.

16. John Murton, "Persecution for Religion Judged and Condemned," in Underhill, 104.

17. Leonard Busher, "Religion's Peace, a Plea for Liberty of Conscience," in Underhill, 25.

18. Bill Bryson, *Shakespeare: The World As a Stage* (London: HarperPerennial, 2007) 8–9.

Chapter 1

Tumultuous Times

17th-century English Baptists in Context

It was hard to be a Baptist in England during the seventeenth century. Then again, the 1600s were hard times for *anyone* to be in England, Baptist or not. In his delightful biography of William Shakespeare, author Bill Bryson pithily describes England near the turn of the seventeenth century as "a world that was short of people and struggled to keep those it had."[1] Recurrent outbreaks of the plague had, over the course of three hundred years, devastated the population. Those who managed to avoid the plague still faced a frightening array of deadly maladies such as tuberculosis, measles, smallpox, and dysentery—threats that were all exacerbated by the unfortunate combination of poor hygiene, unsanitary living conditions, and inadequate diet. By the middle of the seventeenth century, life expectancy in England was forty-eight years old at birth, though people who made it to age thirty could reasonably expect to live another thirty years.[2]

As if these environmental hazards weren't enough for the average person to contend with, the violent political turmoil that had rocked continental Europe throughout the 1500s finally crossed the English Channel in the 1600s. It was, to put it mildly, a tumultuous century. Civil war, regicide, commonwealth, protectorate, restoration, revolution—it all happened between 1642 and 1689, a span of forty-seven years. Little wonder that historian Christopher Hill, a distinguished student of seventeenth-century England, once described these years as "the world turned upside down."³ It was indeed a period of upheaval, and, at the bottom of all this turmoil—or at the top, depending on one's perspective in this upside-down world—was religion.

The "wars of religion" had been raging in Europe since not long after Martin Luther nailed his Ninety-Five Theses to the door of the Castle Church in Wittenberg on 31 October 1517, the first fateful step toward what became the Protestant Reformation. Luther's theological challenge to the Roman Catholic Church also served as the first step toward rearranging political alliances in western Europe. A tug-of-war between sacred and secular powers had been going on, at the very least, since Pope Leo III crowned Charlemagne as "Emperor of the Romans" on Christmas Day in the year 800. At issue was the question of temporal authority. When kings and popes disagreed (as they often did over such issues as taxation, land use, and the appointment of local bishops), who rightfully had the last word? Each side had its advantages, but it was hardly a fair fight. Kings may have had armies at their disposal, but popes wielded an even more frightening weapon: the power to excommunicate the king (and anyone else, for that matter) from the church, which was, in effect, the power to banish the king's soul to eternal damnation. Few monarchs dared to risk the everlasting hounds of hell for the sake of earthly power—and those who did, such as the Holy Roman Emperor, Henry IV, eventually found themselves begging for the pope's forgiveness.⁴

Luther's challenge to the Roman church injected a new element of instability into the old debate. Suddenly, those German princes who had long chafed under the authority of the Holy Roman Empire and the Roman church recognized an opportunity to assert their independence. Fueled as much (if not more) by nationalist sentiment as by theological conviction, they rallied to the reformer's defense and encouraged the establishment of Lutheranism in the territories under their control. This development represented a decisive shift in the relationship between church and state. In the Roman Catholic Church, spiritual unity had transcended political boundaries. Christians in France and England, for example, may have been subjects of different kings, but they were all communicants in the same church.

The rise of Protestantism shattered this unity. Local rulers now claimed the power to decide for themselves which religion would be the established faith—both for themselves and their subjects—in their respective lands, and the map of Europe soon reflected these decisions.[5] Religious identity, in other words, became synonymous with national identity. Faithful worshipers made faithful subjects, and with uniformity came unity. That, at least, was the idea.

What Luther started at Wittenberg spilled over to England in 1534 when Parliament declared King Henry VIII to be supreme head of the Church of England, thus renouncing the authority of the pope and separating England from the Roman Church. While Henry's determination to have his marriage to Catherine of Aragon annulled—and the pope's refusal to grant the annulment—was the specific issue at hand, the king's desire to be rid of unwelcome papal intervention in English affairs of state propelled the separation forward. The subsequent transition in England from a Catholic to a Protestant society was steady but hardly smooth. In the eleven years following Henry's death, the kingdom swung from Protestantism under his heir, Edward VI, back to Catholicism under Mary Tudor, Edward's half-sister, and then back to Protestantism again in 1558 under Elizabeth, Henry's younger daughter. Each swing of the religious pendulum brought with it a great deal of persecutions and reprisals, as those in power did their best to convert (if possible) or destroy (if necessary) those who refused to conform to the new orthodoxy.

Elizabeth's rule put an end to this back-and-forth. Her government, writes historian John Coffey, "was committed to securing religious uniformity, and to achieve that end, it was prepared to employ coercive measures. Its laws and statutes penalized those outside the established church, and although executions for heresy or dissent were rare, fines and imprisonments were common."[6] Elizabeth may have been personally tolerant of religious difference, but she expected her subjects to conform in public. To that end, the Act of Uniformity (1559) imposed a stiff series of penalties for those who deviated from the established doctrines and practices of the Church of England. Catholics were the primary targets of the law, but the ban extended to cover all expressions of religious nonconformity. Scofflaw clergy would earn jail terms of six months, a year, and life, respectively, for their first three offenses. Each violation also carried with it a fine equivalent to a year's income. Lay dissenters paid fines for their first two offenses; a third conviction brought a life sentence in prison. Failure to attend worship, meanwhile, was punishable at a rate of twelve pence per violation.[7] Many more revisions and supplements to the act followed in subsequent years.

Significantly, Coffey argues, the rationale behind these coercive measures enacted under Elizabeth had little to do with religious zealotry and almost everything to do with national security. For the English, he writes, "the historical lesson of Europe's recent religious wars was not that persecution caused strife, but that it was highly dangerous to allow two religions in one territory."[8] From the assumption that religious uniformity was absolutely necessary for the unity of a nation came the related idea that dissenting from the national church was tantamount to dissenting from the nation as a whole. Indeed, those who advocated policies of persecution tended to characterize non-conformists not simply as religious deviants but also, more ominously, as potentially subversive threats to England's national security. In much the same way that extremist Islamic clerics today attract the suspicion of authorities on the lookout for terrorist activity, Coffey notes that "the non-conformist priests could not be treated like men who only sought the spiritual nourishment of their flock. They were dangerous and seditious."[9] Indulgently ignoring these dissenters—and the potential insurgents taking shelter in their congregations—was to court disaster for England. It was, in short, the prospect of disloyalty and treason, not heresy, that made Elizabeth and her successors nervous, particularly in light of the very real threats that England faced in these years from Catholic enemies abroad and Catholic conspirators at home. The record reflects this fearful, defensive preoccupation. While scores of Catholics were hanged for treason during the reigns of Elizabeth and James I, the state only executed eight people during the same period for the specific crimes of either heresy or blasphemy.[10]

Among these eight was a man named Edward Wightman. His primary claim to fame is certainly a dubious distinction: he was the last person to be burned at the stake for heresy in England. He was also a Baptist.[11] A native of Burton-Upon-Trent in the English Midlands, Wightman publicly and repeatedly rejected both the divinity of Jesus and the doctrine of the Trinity. He might have remained little more than Burton-Upon-Trent's eccentric village atheist had he not put his ideas down on paper and sent them to James I as a formal petition. It was a brave move, perhaps, but not very wise. The king referred Wightman and his incriminating petition to the Anglican bishop of Litchfield and Coventry. In addition to his unorthodox opinions about the Godhead, Wightman also had to answer for his refusal to practice baptism (he had called infant baptism "an abominable custom") and the Lord's Supper in the manner prescribed by the Church of England. Not surprisingly, Wightman was convicted of "diverse heresies" by the bishop in December 1611 and turned over to the civil authorities. He was burned alive at Litchfield on 11 April 1612.[12]

Wightman may have been exceptional—the rare heretic in England who was actually executed for heresy—but, as the seventeenth century progressed, religion continued to be intertwined with politics in a way that made being different dangerous. Even within the Church of England, suspicion swirled freely. The so-called Puritans in the church believed that the English Reformation had not gone far enough in jettisoning Catholic rituals, and so they were wary of officials who, with the king's blessing, mandated a strict adherence to the church's formal worship practices. Legalistic enforcement of church rules seemed to them a step in the wrong direction, back toward the Catholicism England had left behind years earlier. Making matters worse for these Puritans, who now held a majority of seats in Parliament, rumors circulated that James's son, Charles I, harbored decidedly Catholic sympathies. Some even claimed he was a Catholic agent—a royal mole, perhaps—intent on delivering the nation back into the hands of the pope.

Relations between king and Parliament grew increasingly tense until matters finally came to a head in 1642, when a struggle for control of the army quickly escalated into civil war.[13] The violence continued intermittently for almost a decade. By the time it ended in September 1651, Charles I had been executed; his son, Charles II, exiled to France; and the English monarchy abolished. In its place, the victorious forces of Parliament established England as a commonwealth. For non-conformists in general—and for Baptists in particular—these tumultuous years of civil war opened the door to an astonishing degree of religious toleration. With the most rigorous enforcers of Anglican orthodoxy remaining loyal to the king, dissenters and other religious radicals had thrown in their lots with Parliament. While some wealthy and influential Baptists helped fund the parliamentary cause, others willingly served as officers and soldiers in Oliver Cromwell's New Model Army. Their support did not go unrecognized or unappreciated.

In a declaration dated 4 March 1647, for example, members of Parliament expressed their dismay over the Baptists' stubborn persistence in differing from established opinion and practice concerning the administration of the ordinances (in other words, their refusal to baptize infants). "Yet herein we hold it fit," the declaration read, "that men should be convinced by the word of God with great gentleness and reason, and not beaten out of [their errors] by force and violence."[14] For Baptists used to facing jail time and exorbitant fines as punishments for practicing their faith, such restraint was as welcome as it was unprecedented. To be sure, strong legal measures against dissent remained on the books, even if they were not enforced as rigorously as they had been in the past. Toleration, after all, was not the same thing as freedom. Baptists were still considered the equivalent of second-class citizens. They were not, however, actively persecuted during these years, a development that represented a definite step in the right direction.

In part, the relatively tolerant religious atmosphere of the day was a matter of political expediency. It also, however, reflected the personal convictions of Cromwell, the military leader who became Lord Protector of the English Commonwealth in 1653. While his own religious commitments were vague, Cromwell had little patience for intolerance. As a general, he had chosen his officers based on the strength of their characters and the depth of their religious convictions. *That* they believed, in other words, was to Cromwell more important than *what* they believed, as long as what they believed fell within the boundaries of a loosely defined Protestantism. One historian has described his New Model Army as "an alliance bound together by a common interest in liberty of conscience."[15] Upon assuming the title of Lord Protector, one of Cromwell's first orders of business was to announce that, henceforth, "such as profess faith in God by Christ Jesus, though differing in judgment from the doctrine, worship, or discipline publicly held forth should not be restrained from, but protected in, the profession of their faith and exercise of their religion." It's worth noting, though, that Cromwell did attach a qualifier to this remarkable pronouncement of toleration: non-conformists should "abuse not this liberty to the civil injury of others and the actual disturbance of the public peace."[16] The old habit of linking religious uniformity with civil harmony—or, conversely, disloyalty with dissent—was hard to break, even for a committed tolerationist such as Cromwell.

Nevertheless, the contrast with England's recent past was stunning. During these Interregnum years—that is, the period between the execution of Charles I and the restoration of Charles II—English religion was, writes Coffey, "largely deregulated, and monopoly gave way to an unprecedented measure of free trade." The only traders not officially tolerated were Catholics and high church Anglicans, "both of whom were suspected of wanting to re-establish their own lost monopolies."[17] In this freer-than-before market, radical groups such as the Baptists enjoyed the opportunity to spread their ideas and win new converts. After struggling mightily to survive the harsh environment of the early 1600s, Baptists in England began to gain some much-needed traction by mid-century—still on the margins of society, but no longer the target of regular, legally sanctioned harassment. In this season of relative ease, however, the old prejudices never completely disappeared. Looking back at the Interregnum thirty years later, Thomas Grantham could still recall being dragged "before the judgment seats because we would not worship God after the will of the Lord Protector—for so they styled him in their articles against us. And we had our goods taken away and never restored to this day."[18] Unfortunately for Grantham and his fellow Baptists, with the end of the Protectorate and the return of Charles II, this kind of treatment would soon come to seem mild by comparison.

When Oliver Cromwell died, he was succeeded as Lord Protector by his son Richard, who possessed neither the charisma nor the credentials nor (perhaps most important) the talent to be an effective leader. After only nine months in the position, Richard Cromwell resigned as Lord Protector in 1659, and, at the urging of the army, a newly elected Parliament convened in April 1660 to settle the matter of how—and by whom—England should be governed. Six days after the beginning of these deliberations, a letter arrived from Charles II, who for almost ten years had been waiting in exile for just this moment. In the letter, commonly referred to as the Declaration of Breda, after the Dutch town from which it was sent, Charles somewhat grandly invited his former subjects to "return to their duty" under their rightful king and, as a sign of his good intentions, offered full pardons for past political offenses and a guarantee of religious toleration. "We do declare a liberty to tender consciences," the presumptive monarch wrote, in terms similar to Oliver Cromwell's proclamation of 1653, "and [declare] that no man should be disquieted, or called into question, for differences of opinion in matters of religion which do not disturb the general peace of the kingdom."[19]

Despite objections from some of its more skeptical members, Parliament chose to take Charles at his word and voted to recall him from exile, trusting that he would keep the generous promises he had made at Breda. It was, as one historian ruefully put it, "a confidence of which all parties soon has sufficient reason to repent."[20] The problem was that Charles had shrewdly hedged his bets by insisting his liberal assurances be secured not as royal indulgences but rather by acts of Parliament. In other words, the king could declare that these were his intentions, but it was up to Parliament to make them reality. Charles landed in Dover on 26 May 1660 and triumphantly entered London as king three days later. The old order swiftly reasserted itself, sweeping away the more tolerant religious regulations that had governed England during the Interregnum and resurrecting the Elizabethan statutes calling for the persecution of non-conformists.

That was bad enough. In January 1661, however, fifty so-called "Fifth Monarchists," a group of non-conformist radicals convinced that the second coming of Christ was imminent, launched an ill-fated attempt to conquer London in the name of King Jesus, the first step in a wider plot to overthrow the government of Charles II. The Fifth Monarchy Men were inspired by the ideas of John Archer, an radical preacher exiled in Amsterdam, who, through a series of calculations based on the biblical books of Daniel and Revelation, had prophesied that around 1700, Jesus would return to the earth and establish his personal rule—what Archer called the fifth monarchy (the previous four being the empires of Babylon, Persia, Alexander the Great, and Rome). These apocalyptic ideas had been circulating in England since at least the early 1640s and were particularly appealing to a number of high-ranking officers in Oliver Cromwell's army, including Thomas Harrison, the military commander-in-chief of England. Following the collapse of the protectorate and return of Charles II, the Fifth Monarchy Men, with Harrison in the lead, continued their underground campaign to prepare the way for Lord Jesus' return. When Harrison was executed in 1660 for his role in the death of Charles I, a wine-barrel maker named Thomas Venner stepped up to replace him. The January uprising lasted three days. When it was over, Venner and his band of around fifty followers had thoroughly terrorized London, killed twenty-two people, and ignited a full-scale panic in the government. Venner was hanged, drawn, and quartered for high treason.

More far-reaching consequences swiftly followed. On 10 January 1661, the king issued an order forbidding Anabaptists, Quakers, and Fifth Monarchists from gathering to worship, except in churches or private homes—and even then their numbers were restricted. The suspicion, of course, was that these non-conformist "worship services" were actually secret meetings, or "conventicles," of wild-eyed religious radicals determined to overthrow the government. More extensive crackdowns seemed inevitable. Indeed, before Venner's adventure, chances were slim that Parliament would turn

Charles's Breda promises into law. Less than two months before the Fifth Monarchy outburst, in fact, Parliament had narrowly defeated an effort to do just that. In the aftermath of the failed rebellion, however, it soon became clear that this Parliament (nicknamed the "Cavalier Parliament" because of its strong support for the monarchy and the old established church order) was hardly in the mood to pardon the past and encourage religious diversity. After all, had not recent events, from the years of civil war to the Fifth Monarchy uprising, proven in dramatic, bloody fashion that non-conformity and rebellion—dissent from the church and disloyalty to the king—went hand in hand?

Referring to the language of the Breda Declaration, Baptist historian B. R. White writes that, because "'differences in matters of religion' were judged by a majority in Parliament from 1661 onwards inevitably to 'disturb the general peace of the kingdom,' dissenters of any kind, whether Protestant or Roman Catholic, could only expect serious trouble."[21] The Corporation Act (1661) excluded non-conformists from public service by requiring all elected officials to swear an oath of allegiance and receive the Lord's Supper according to the rites of the Church of England within a year of their election. The Act of Uniformity (1662) established the Book of Common Prayer as the only legitimate standard for worship in the kingdom and required that all Christian ministers not only be ordained in the Church of England but also profess their assent to all doctrines, rituals, and practices prescribed in the prayer book as well. The Conventicle Act (1664) turned Charles's earlier royal order against non-conformist meetings into law, resurrecting the old Elizabethan statues that required church attendance and banning all religious services that did not proceed according to the Church of England's liturgy. The act empowered local sheriffs and magistrates to disrupt and disband illegal meetings and arrest those in attendance. After a third offense, adult men faced a choice of banishment "to some American plantation for seven years" or a fine of one hundred pounds.[22] Meanwhile, married women arrested at these conventicles could spend up to a year in jail unless their husbands paid a fine of forty shillings to secure their release. Finally, the Five-Mile Act

(1665) banned non-conformist ministers from coming within five miles of any incorporated town.

Together, these laws were known as the Clarendon Code, named after the Earl of Clarendon, who, as Lord Chancellor for Charles II, was responsible for their enforcement. The code reflected the nation's reactionary mood following the Restoration. Indeed, after nearly twenty years of almost continuous social, political, and religious upheaval, there was, among the English gentry, a desperate desire for stability, and a determination, as it were, to stuff the genie of chaos back into the radical lamp from which it had sprung. Local magistrates, who tended to come from the ranks of aristocratic landowners, zealously enforced the new laws, which were increasingly draconian and allowed little patience with any kind of activity that hinted at disloyalty to the king. The Clarendon Code represented, as one historian put it, a systematic response to widespread insecurity about the supposed connections between political radicalism and religious dissent that threatened to undermine the stability of both the English church and the English state. It was, in other words, a kind of Patriot Act for the seventeenth century, designed to curtail the "dangerous practices of seditious sectaries and other disloyal persons who under pretense of tender consciences do at their meetings connive insurrections."[23] Charles II may have returned to England preaching religious toleration, but his nearly twenty-four-year reign there was marked—some would even say defined—by what one historian has called "the calculated and often malicious persecution of dissent."[24]

The seventeenth century, in short, was a bad time to be different in England. And yet these were the years in which the Baptists emerged there as a distinct group of dissenting Christians. At times during this tumultuous and dangerous century, they flourished in the midst of all the chaos. More often, however, they struggled to eke out a precarious existence on the margins of society—especially in an anxious climate where religious dissent smelled suspiciously like political disloyalty. The Baptists struggled, but they refused to go away. Instead, they stubbornly insisted that it was indeed possible to be, at the same time, a faithful disciple of Jesus, a loyal subject of the king, an obedient reader of the Bible, and a respecter of individual conscience. That was their distinctive Christian witness—and it is to them, these seventeenth-century English Baptists who lived in interesting times, that we now turn our full attention.

The record shows that there had been Christians practicing believers' baptism—or, Anabaptists—in England since before 1550, most (if not all) of them foreigners and most (if not all) of them either banished or burned on account of their religious beliefs. Since the word "Anabaptist" was used at that time as a generic designation for any brand of non-conforming, irregular, or fanatical religious persuasion, it is difficult to pinpoint with any real precision the identities of these various Anabaptists when they appear in the history books.[25] "Anabaptist" means, literally, "baptized again," and originally referred to Christians who, rejecting their infant baptism as somehow inauthentic or invalid, insisted on being re-baptized as adult believers.

The word had, for several decades, been associated with various heresies in Europe before it became infamous in 1534 as a result of the Münster Rebellion. Led by a man named John of Leiden, a group of radical Anabaptists seized control of the German city of Münster, renamed it "New Jerusalem," banned all private property and books (except the Bible), legalized polygamy, and hunkered down to await the Second Coming of Jesus. Jesus, however, did not come, and in 1535, Münster was retaken by an army led by the town's Lutheran bishop. John and other leading citizens of New Jerusalem were publicly tortured and executed, and then—with a particularly gruesome sixteenth-century flourish—their corpses placed in cages and hoisted to hang atop the steeple of St. Lambert's Church in the city center. The corpses are long gone, but the cages hang there still, a stark reminder of this exercise in Anabaptist anarchy.

Not surprisingly, the Münster episode gave the Anabaptist movement a dangerous reputation for radicalism and revolution that it found almost impossible to shed. In fact, for years to come, "Münster" served as an all-purpose epithet used to discredit any group of Christians who practiced believers' baptism. One never could be too sure of what these re-baptizers were up to: what their intentions were, where their true loyalties lay, or when they might try again to overturn the social order. After all, remember what happened at Münster? It was an effective smear. Separatists in England, for example, steadfastly maintained that, because the Anglican Church had departed from the biblical pattern for congregational life found in the New Testament, it could not be considered a true church. Yet, despite their convictions, these Separatists could not bring themselves to take the logical next step of repudiating the baptism they had received as infants from the Church of England.[26] They believed—in ways contemporary readers can scarcely imagine—that infant baptism tied church and community together into an organic, ordered whole. Rejecting infant baptism (as the Anabaptists in Münster had done, with disastrous results) put the entire established social order at risk. Münster cast a long shadow indeed.

Undeterred by such fears and finally persuaded by the example of believers' baptism found in the New Testament, a man named John Smyth took the bold step in 1609 of baptizing first himself, and then the rest of his little congregation of English Separatists living in Amsterdam. In contrast to the elaborate rituals that marked worship in the Church of England, these Baptists (as they soon became known) in Amsterdam worshiped very simply, and they did so, they believed, in keeping with the pattern established by 1 Corinthians 14:30-31. Writing to relatives in England, two members of Smyth's church described their typical Sunday schedule. According to Hugh Bromstead and his wife, "morning exercises" began at eight, with a chapter or two of Scripture read aloud in preparation for worship. Then they awaited "the spontaneous outpouring of the Holy Spirit through prophesying," as the Bible was laid aside and a preacher began to expound upon a particular text for forty-five minutes to an hour. The first sermon would be followed by perhaps up to four more "as time will give leave," until the morning session came to a close with prayer and a collection for the poor. They returned at two in the afternoon to do it all over again, with another three to four hours of prophesying, before ending the day's spiritual exercises with a discussion of church business.[27]

Thus the Baptist movement started in Amsterdam. The specific details—the who, what, when, and where—of these beginnings have been told elsewhere and need not be recounted here.[28] What *should* be recounted, however, are the principles that moved Smyth and his congregation to make their decisive break with religious convention. The early Baptists, wrote British historian E. B. Underhill in 1846, held four basic convictions about the Christian faith that put them at odds with the religious establishment in England. They believed that "the church of God must be a community of holy men" (that is to say, people who confess a faith in Jesus Christ, are baptized on the basis of that confession, and live in obedience to Jesus' commands); that "faith is the result of divine tuition alone and cannot be compelled by fire or sword"; that "a rite that has neither the sanction nor the command of the Lord Jesus Christ or his apostles must not be admitted among the ordinances of the Lord's house"; and, finally, that "secular potentates have neither place nor dominion in the kingdom of him who is the blessed and only Potentate, the King of kings and Lord of lords. As there is but one Lord, there is but one lawgiver in the church, Jesus Christ."[29] Every single one of these principles, of course, represented a dramatic departure from the doctrines of the Anglican Church, which routinely baptized infants, coerced religious conformity, practiced worship rituals not found in Scripture, and recognized the English monarch as its legitimate "potentate."

Not surprisingly, then, the Baptists in England almost immediately ran into trouble following their return from Amsterdam in 1612. Their leader, Thomas Helwys, wrote a remarkable defense of religious liberty—not only for Christians but also for all people of all religious persuasions—and, just as Edward Wightman did at about the same time, he sent an autographed copy of his work to the king. For his trouble, Helwys was thrown in jail, where he languished until his death.[30] As we shall see, Helwys was not the only Baptist to spend time in jail for the crime of non-conformity. There was, to be sure, a price to pay for identifying with an outlawed movement of religious dissenters in an age of great anxiety and insecurity. For the next twenty-five years after Helwys's death, writes historian B. R. White, Baptists in England "could only manage to maintain a precarious underground existence."[31] In 1626, one London congregation reportedly had 150 members, but it was by far the exception. Other churches in the cities of Coventry, Lincoln, Salisbury, and Tiverton were much smaller.[32] By the time Charles II returned to the throne in 1660, there were, by one estimate, around 240 Baptist congregations in all of England. Of these, roughly 130 were General Baptist churches, with the remainder being Particular Baptist.[33]

At this point, a brief word about the difference between the General and Particular Baptists is perhaps in order. The General Baptists, the older of the two branches, were the spiritual descendants of the earliest Baptists in Amsterdam. As their name suggests, they held a general view of the atonement, believing that Jesus died for the sake of all people. Particular Baptist congregations, meanwhile, emerged in England during the 1630s and took a particular, or limited, view of atonement, maintaining that Jesus died only for those individuals chosen by God for salvation. Their understandings of atonement differed—as did their views on the ordained ministry and the possibility of cooperation among individual congregations—but they agreed that the true church of Christ rightly consisted only of those who had come to faith and then been baptized as believers. In other words, a true church could not be made up of individuals baptized as infants. As such, Baptists of both persuasions, General and Particular, were equally offensive to the established religious and cultural sensibilities of seventeenth-century England.[34]

And from whence did these early Baptists get all their scandalous ideas? Well, the simple answer is that they got them from the Bible. It's no exaggeration to say that, for Baptists in seventeenth-century England, Scripture represented not merely *one* source of authority among many. Instead, it stood alone as *the* authority. "What things are chiefly contained in the Holy Scriptures?" asked Particular Baptist pastor Benjamin Keach in his *Baptist Catechism* of 1677. The answer left no wiggle room: "The Holy Scriptures chiefly contain what man ought to believe concerning God and what duty God requireth of man."[35] Simply put, wrote Thomas Grantham, a General Baptist, in 1662, there is no higher authority than the "Holy Text."[36]

As we shall explore further in the next chapter, this kind of wholesale submission to Scripture might seem odd, or even a bit naïve, to those of us who live on *this* side of the Enlightenment, that period of Western history, roughly 1650 to 1800, in which people came to the conclusion that human reason, if properly and rigorously applied, could provide explanations for the universe and our place in it. At one time, those sorts of big-picture issues had been left for theologians and philosophers to sort out. In the age of Enlightenment, however, they became subjects for scientific investigation. If something could be proven according to the supposedly objective standards of science, then it was a *fact*. If it couldn't, then it was a matter of subjective *opinion*. Facts were *true*. Opinions were . . . well, something else. Everyone, of course, *had* opinions, but they were just that: opinions, which meant that they carried no objective authority. Because its truth claims fell outside the boundaries of what could be scientifically proven, therefore, religion gradually drifted into the realm of opinion during the age of Enlightenment and afterwards.

This shift in thinking brought with it a shift in how people read and understood the Bible. In the wake of the Enlightenment, any authority that a "holy text" might have for an individual, or for a community of individuals, was assumed to be wholly generated by the individual or community. The text could not be true in any absolute sense because it lay beyond the realm of fact. Is the Bible true? To the Enlightenment mindset, the very question itself was a *non sequitur*, akin to asking whether a beagle should properly be considered a long- or short-haired cat. Contemporary readers of Scripture may come to the text and say, "That's all well and good, but we *must* take other factors into consideration as well if we really want to get to the truth of it." This kind of skepticism is a legacy of the Enlightenment and is the burden of contemporary readers. It was most definitely not a burden that Baptists in seventeenth-century England carried with them when they opened their Bibles.

Indeed, as White points out, the authority of Scripture was an assumption for the early Baptists in the same way that fish assume water. The Bible, he writes, reveals God's truth in all matters of faith and practice, including the nature of the church. In the New

Testament's description of the apostolic church, furthermore, Baptists believed there was sufficient enough evidence to enable any later generation of Christians to reconstruct the church in accordance with the original pattern—which was, according to the New Testament, plainly a believer's church.[37] Moreover, White writes, "this concern for the reconstitution of the apostolic model explains why, in so many Baptist documents, the argument was considered incomplete without Scripture references. In all their arguments, debates, and struggles, they were trying to discover what was the will of God and then to bring their practice, for example, about baptism, church worship, the laying on of hands, the payment of tithes, the ministry, or their duty to the state into conformity with that will."[38]

Unfortunately for these conscientious readers of Scripture (but perhaps providentially so for their spiritual descendants) the persecutions of the tumultuous seventeenth century afforded plenty of opportunities for Baptists to articulate, defend, and share their faith convictions in the public square. Of particular concern for hard-pressed Baptists during these years was, not surprisingly, religious toleration—or, more to the point, the failure of the English king to secure the kind of religious toleration that Jesus and the apostles so clearly modeled in the New Testament. It was indeed dangerous in those days to dissent from established church doctrines and practices, and breathless historical accounts of Baptist resistance to oppressive religious laws and overzealous persecutors sometimes read like swashbuckling cliffhangers. In his nineteenth-century history of the English Baptists, for example, Adam Taylor told the story of twelve Baptists—ten men, two women—arrested in Aylesbury, Buckinghamshire, and convicted of holding an illegal secret meeting in 1663.[39] After a morning trial, they were given the choice of either publicly renouncing their non-conformist beliefs or being sent into exile from England. Otherwise, they would be sentenced to death.

The twelve Baptists were given until the afternoon to make their decision. When afternoon came, all twelve refused to accept either penalty and threw themselves on the mercy of the court, which immediately handed them over to the executioner and ordered their property to be seized. Upon hearing the news, a son of one of the prisoners jumped on a horse and rode off to London, some fifty miles away, to try to find a way to stop the executions. He located William Kiffin, who was the pastor of a Baptist congregation in London—and, unusually for Baptists in the seventeenth century, well connected with people who had access to the king. Kiffin knew the Lord Chancellor and asked him to request the king's intervention. Surprised by what was going on in Buckinghamshire, Charles II issued an emergency reprieve, which was quickly drawn up, signed, and delivered to the prisoner's son, who rode furiously back to Aylesbury, hoping to make it back before the executioner carried out the twelve death sentences. He just did make it. "Upon his arrival," wrote Taylor, "the news of his success diffused a general joy among the non-conformists . . . [and] filled their persecutors with dismay."[40]

While perhaps more dramatic than most, Taylor's story reflects the reality of religious persecution in seventeenth-century England. It happened, probably more frequently than we're aware of. And when it happened, when they were harassed or jailed for violating the laws requiring religious conformity, early English Baptists responded to this rough treatment not with the sword but with the pen. They wrote. They petitioned. They published. And when they did, they grounded their arguments against persecution—and for toleration—not in anything as abstract as human rights (the modern form of which, really, had yet to be invented and popularized) but, rather, in the word of God as revealed specifically in the Bible. They read the New Testament, applied what they found to their own circumstances, and staked out their positions accordingly. We are the beneficiaries of the written legacies they left behind.

Now, it must be said that among these early English Baptists, some, such as Thomas Helwys, went so far as to call for religious liberty—that is, a complete freedom for individuals to practice (or not to practice) their faith as they are led by their consciences. Religious liberty also demands that a person's religious convictions (or, again, lack thereof) have no bearing on his or her status as a citizen or subject. Simply put, there is no such thing as a second-class citizenship for those who do not practice the officially established religion because there is no such thing as an officially established religion.

Many more Baptists in seventeenth-century England, however, argued passionately for religious toleration, which is not the same as religious liberty. Toleration recognizes that there is, indeed, an officially established religion (the Church of England, for example), but, at the same time, it does not prohibit individuals from practicing their own religions within boundaries set by the government. A religiously tolerant government might say, "There are no penalties for non-conformity, but we won't let non-conformists hold public office." In other words, toleration acknowledges that differences of religion may affect a person's status as a citizen or a subject.

From the relative comfort of a twenty-first-century Western democracy in which religious liberty is written into the law of the land, it can be tempting to classify as full-blooded Baptist heroes only those who pressed for religious liberty, while ignoring those who argued for the more limited virtue of toleration as somehow less brave or less bold. This sort of discrimination, however, is mistaken. The seventeenth century was a difficult time to be a Baptist in England. It took a great deal of courage to follow the leadership of conscience and be different. It took even more courage to articulate these differences in public and in writing. For dissenters who were being relentlessly persecuted for their faith—and paying for their dissent with their liberty and their property—toleration represented a huge relief and a giant step in the right direction, not a failure of vision or nerve. Contemporary Baptists owe their spiritual forebears a tremendous debt for their willingness to stand firm on their faith convictions, regardless of whether they argued for religious liberty or for religious toleration.

The debt does not end there. In their pamphlets and petitions, these faithful Baptists also left a rich body of work that collectively stands, four hundred years later, as an example of how to articulate Christian convictions in the public square in a distinctively Christian way, a skill that many of us have allowed to atrophy. With the turbulent 1600s as a backdrop, then, it is time to begin reading the Bible with our Baptist ancestors—and the first thing we discover is that, even in the seventeenth century, where people begin their reading of Scripture makes all the difference in where they end up.

Notes

1. Bill Bryson, *Shakespeare: The World As a Stage* (London: HarperPerennial, 2007) 22.

2. Jeffery L. Singman, *Daily Life in Elizabethan England* (Westport CT: Greenwood Press, 1995) 51.

3. See Christopher Hill, *The World Turned Upside Down: Radical Ideas During the English Revolution* (London: Penguin Books, 1972) for a thorough, readable survey of seventeenth-century English political and religious radicalism.

4. The conflict between Henry IV and Pope Gregory VII is perhaps the most famous pre-Reformation showdown between sacred and secular powers. When Gregory moved to reclaim from the Holy Roman emperor the church's right to name its own bishops, Henry refused to concede. Gregory responded by excommunicating him. Finally, in January 1077, Henry walked barefoot through the snow to seek Gregory's forgiveness at a fortress in Canossa. While politically motivated on Henry's part, the act of submission served as a vivid demonstration of papal power and burned an indelible—and humiliating—image onto the collective memory of Europe's rulers. See Kenneth Scott LaTourette, *Beginnings to 1500*, vol. 1 of A History of Christianity (San Francisco: HarperCollins, 1975) 470–73.

5. For a nice overview of this turbulent period, see Justo L. Gonzales, *The Reformation to the Present Day* , vol. 2 of The Story of Christianity (San Francisco: HarperCollins, 1985) 38–93.

6. John Coffey, *Persecution and Toleration in Protestant England, 1558–1689* (Harlow, England: Longman, 2000) 11. Coffey's book is an excellent resource for understanding not only *what* happened during this period of persecution in England but also *why* it happened.

7. Coffey, *Persecution and Toleration in Protestant England*, 83.

8. Ibid., 38.

9. Ibid.

10. Under the devoutly Catholic Mary, Coffey observes, Protestants were burned at the stake for heresy. Hers was an aggressive religious persecution to stamp out false doctrine. Under the more casually Protestant Elizabeth, more than two hundred Catholics were hanged at the gallows for treason, suggesting a reactive campaign motivated more out of fear than faith (see Coffey, 85ff).

11. Joseph Ivimey, *A History of English Baptists*, vol. 1 (London: Burditt, Button et al., 1811) 123. Coffey identifies Wightman as a more radical Anabaptist (114–15).

12. Ivimey, *History of English Baptists*, 123–24.

13. For a nice summary of the events that precipitated the English Civil War, see Michael R. Watts, *The Dissenters: From the Reformation to the French Revolution* (Oxford: Clarendon Press, 1978) 77ff.

14. Adam Taylor, *The History of the English General Baptists*, vol. 1 (London: T. Bore, 1818) 121–22.

15. Watts, *The Dissenters*, 107.

16. Taylor, *History of the English General Baptists*, 127.

17. Coffey, *Persecution and Toleration in Protestant England*, 160.

18. Grantham, quoted in J. W. Wood, *A Condensed History of the General Baptists of the New Connexion* (London: Simpkin, Marshall, and Co., 1847) 124.

19. From the Declaration of Breda, as found in Earl of Clarendon, *The History of the Rebellion and Civil Wars in England*, ed. W. D. McCray, vol. 6 (Oxford: Clarendon Press, 1888) 206ff.

20. Taylor, *History of the English General Baptists*, 174.

21. B. R. White, *The English Baptists of the 17th Century* (Didcot: The Baptist Historical Society, 1983; repr., 1996) 95.

22. Taylor, *History of the English General Baptists*, 180.

23. Anthony Fletcher, "The Enforcement of the Conventicle Acts, 1664–1679," in *Persecution and Toleration*, ed. W. J. Sheils (Oxford: Basil Blackwell, 1984) 236.

24. Watts, *The Dissenters*, 222.

25. Champlain Burrage, *The Early English Dissenters*, vol. 1 (Cambridge: Cambridge University Press, 1912) 41.

26. See Watts, *The Dissenters*, 44.

27. As quoted in Burrage, *The Early English Dissenters*, vol. 1, 236.

28. The two standard histories of the Baptist movement are Robert G. Torbet, *A History of the Baptists* (Philadelphia: Judson Press, 1950) and H. Leon McBeth, *The Baptist Heritage* (Nashville: Broadman Press, 1987). Either may be consulted with confidence.

29. E. B. Underhill, *Tracts of Liberty of Conscience and Persecution, 1614–1661* (London: J. Haddon, 1846) lxxiv.

30. We don't know exactly when Helwys died, but we do know that he was most certainly dead by 1616, when his uncle, Geoffrey, bequeathed a legacy of £10 to his widow, Joan. See A. C. Underwood, *A History of the English Baptists* (London: Kingsgate Press, 1947) 48.

31. White, *English Baptists of the 17th Century*, 23.

32. Coffey, Persecution and Toleration in Protestant England, 113.

33. Watts, *The Dissenters*, 160.

34. For an extended discussion about the differences between the General and Particular Baptists, see White, *English Baptists of the 17th Century*, 9ff. See also the entries for each community in William Brackney, *Historical Dictionary of the Baptists* (Lanham MD: The Scarecrow Press, Ltd., 1999).

35. Benjamin Keach, *The Baptist Catechism, or A Brief Instruction in the Principles of Christian Religion*, 16th ed. (London: John Robinson, 1764) 7.

36. Thomas Grantham, *The Prisoner Against the Prelate, or A Dialogue Between the Common Gaol and Cathedral of Lincoln* (n.p., 1662) 74.

37. White, *English Baptists of the 17th Century*, 12.

38. Ibid., 13.

39. Taylor, *History of the English General Baptists*, 226ff.

40. Ibid., 229.

Chapter 2

Reading Scripture with 17th-century English Baptists

A Brief Primer

People who read a text carefully and conscientiously may very well arrive at different interpretations of what they have read. This observation is hardly earth shaking. It is akin to noting that water is wet, fire is hot, and ice is cold. Whether we're discussing the plays of Shakespeare, the poetry of Eliot, the lyrics of Lennon and McCartney, the definition of the strike zone, or the fine print of an insurance policy, we take it for granted that intelligent, reasonable individuals can read the exact same material and yet understand it in a wide variety of ways. The Bible is no exception. In good faith and with good will, Christians (and non-Christians, for that matter) can read the same passage of Scripture and come to different conclusions about its meaning, a fact that often gets obscured when we announce our intention to stake out *the* biblical position on a particular subject.

Acknowledging the plain reality of such diversity, of course, is hardly the same thing as denying the existence of absolute biblical truth. At our best, Baptists approach Scripture with humility, relying on the Holy Spirit for guidance in getting it right, while at the same time confessing that sin still retains enough power over us to cloud our judgment and guarantee the possibility that we might get it wrong. As Paul suggests in 1 Corinthians 13:12, the fact that we can only partially grasp the fullness of God's truth right now says more about us than it says about God's truth. In other words, different *interpretations* of Scripture do not call the essential *truth* of Scripture into question. It endures, regardless of whether we have arrived at the point of understanding correctly it or not. After all, the moon existed long before Neil Armstrong first stepped onto its surface.

While some Christians still insist that there is but one simple, clear meaning of Scripture that should be readily apparent to anyone capable of opening a Bible and reading it, the reality is a bit more complicated. When it comes to matters of biblical interpretation, where we end up depends largely on where we begin. Consider, by way of analogy, the manner in which United States Supreme Court justices interpret the Constitution. Broadly speaking, there are two basic approaches to this important task, each one shaped by a different philosophical understanding of the law. Justices who adhere to the idea of "original intent" believe that, when presented with a specific legal issue, their job is to go back to the relevant portion of the Constitution and, through a close reading of the text, discern as accurately as they can what the framers had in mind when they wrote it so that the current issue in question can be resolved in accordance with the framers' intentions. Justices who consider the Constitution to be a "living document," meanwhile, are interested in distilling general principles from the written text that can then serve as basic, but elastic, guidelines for deciding issues the framers could never have anticipated. Simply put, "original intent" advocates insist that the text of the Constitution—and thus, by default, the men who wrote it—should always get the last word in the decision-making process, while those who promote a "living document" understand the text itself as the starting point for principled judicial reflection by contemporary minds in the context of current events. All nine justices read the same Constitution carefully, thoughtfully, and with integrity, but the philosophical approach they each bring to the text cannot help shaping the outcome of their deliberations. The conclusions they end up with are driven, in large part, by the assumptions with which they begin.

Biblical scholars use a fancy word to describe the various approaches people take to the task of interpreting Scripture. *Hermeneutics* refers to the way we read a given text: the assumptions we bring with us, the prejudices we hold, the perspective from which we look at a given passage—really, anything that affects the way we understand what we read. Each of the two judicial philosophies outlined above, for example, represents a particular hermeneutical approach to interpreting the Constitution. Likewise, when reading the Bible, it is important to acknowledge that all of us do so under the influence of a certain hermeneutic. We usually fail to recognize it as such because our particular way of reading seems perfectly normal and natural to us, in much the same way that none of us think we speak with an accent. The truth is, just as we all have accents that give our speech its distinctive sound, we all have hermeneutics that give our interpretation of Scripture its distinctive perspective.

Need an example? Consider the way Christians interpret Isaiah 53. Most of us, when we read this passage, instinctively assume that Isaiah is referring to Jesus. That assumption, then, shapes the way we interpret the passage as a prophetic anticipation of how the Son of God will suffer pain, humiliation, and indignity for our sake without protesting or retaliating against his tormentors. We read the Isaiah text and, mentally, we fast-forward to the New Testament's passion narratives and connect the prophet's description of the Lord's servant with Matthew, Mark, Luke, and John's accounts of what happened to Jesus. Nothing in these verses from Isaiah specifically mentions Jesus—or even the Son of God—but we assume that, given what we believe to be true about Jesus, he *must* be the one to whom Isaiah is referring. When we interpret Isaiah 53 in this fashion, we are taking a specific hermeneutical approach to the text, one that, say, an Orthodox Jew—for whom Isaiah 53 is also Holy Scripture—would not.[1] It's worth repeating: when trying to understand Scripture, our conclusions about what we have read are largely shaped by the assumptions we bring with us to the text.

Hermeneutics matter, especially when reading Scripture across time and space with our seventeenth-century English Baptist ancestors. Understanding their approach to the Bible will help us better understand why they responded as they did to what they read. Moreover, they can, perhaps, teach us a hermeneutical approach to reading the Bible that will enable us to become more articulate and persuasive advocates for religious liberty, comfortable discussing this distinctive faith conviction of ours in unapologetically biblical terms. Unlike today, when few—if any—Christians turn *first* to Scripture for guidance when talking about the intersection of freedom and faith, English Baptists in the 1600s found themselves pushing against a long tradition that was, to some extent, also grounded in the reading of Scripture, but from a very different perspective. Indeed, as has been said before, the devil can quote the Bible to suit his purposes, and in the first millennium and a half of Christian history, biblical precedent figured heavily in bolstering arguments intended to justify religious persecution. Hermeneutics matter. So, if we want to read Scripture with the seventeenth-century English Baptists, then we need to develop an appreciation of how they read it—and the ways in which their hermeneutical approach differed from that of other Christians trying, in their own way and according to their own interpretation of Scripture, to bring theological order to the confusing reality of religious diversity.

Indeed, by the seventeenth century, proponents of religious persecution had been diligently sifting through the Scriptures for well over a thousand years in search of a biblical answer to the nagging question of what to do with religious non-conformists. When the Roman emperor Constantine converted to Christianity in the fourth century, the church experienced a sudden and dramatic reversal of fortunes, going from a minority sect without any influence to an established religion backed by all the earthly power of the world's greatest empire. Looking back, Baptists and other advocates of religious toleration pinpointed this so-called "Constantinian shift" as the moment when Christianity, as practiced in the New Testament, lost its way and became a persecuting faith.[2] Whether motivated by political considerations, religious scruples, or probably some combination of both, emperors from the fourth century onward regularly used their coercive power to enforce orthodox theology and punish heresy. Their intervention was not only welcomed by church officials—it was encouraged.

Impressed by what he saw as the remarkably positive effects of coercion in his hometown of Hippo during the Donatist controversy, for example, Augustine wrote a series of letters in the early 400s that offered a theological justification for persecution as a kind of tragically necessary tough love, meted out in this world for the purpose of saving heretics from the pain of eternal damnation in the next.[3] Subsequent theologians during the Middle Ages and beyond, including Thomas Aquinas, built on the foundation laid by Augustine.[4] This Christian tradition of persecution not only survived the Reformation but was also endorsed by both Martin Luther and John Calvin.[5] (Ironically enough, as the practice of persecution evolved, its scope narrowed, excluding those outside the Christian fold, such as Jews and Muslims. By the strange logic of persecution, non-Christians could be tolerated by virtue of their ignorance, but non-conforming Christians could not, presumably because they knew better and were therefore accountable for their deviant behavior.[6])

The Christian tradition of persecution may have rested on theological arguments originally made by Augustine, but it was buttressed through the years by a reading of Scripture that emphasized the Old Testament, particularly the unique relationship between God and the nation of Israel. Magisterial reformers such as Calvin, for example, considered Israel to be a universally applicable model for a divinely ordered society.[7] They found support for this view in texts such as Psalm 2, in which the LORD invests his chosen king with authority over the nations and the power "to crush them with a sceptre of iron, and break them in pieces like a potter's vessel" (Ps 2:9). Moreover, the psalm continues, the rulers of this earth must be advised: "Serve the LORD in fear, and rejoice in trembling. Kiss the Son, lest he be angry and you perish in the way; when his wrath shall suddenly burn, blessed are all that trust in him" (Ps 2:10-11). Earthly rulers not only had to obey God's law themselves but also had both a divine right and a responsibility to ensure that their subjects did likewise.[8] Herein lay a biblical justification both for an established, national religion and for the use of force to ensure religious conformity.

Indeed, the Old Testament abounds with examples of earthly authorities taking coercive, often violent, measures against false worship and idolatry. In Exodus 32:25-28, Moses instructs the Levites to take up swords to kill three thousand Israelites as punishment for their worship of a golden bull. In 1 Kings 19:40, the prophet Elijah orders the priests of Ba'al to be slaughtered at the brook of Kidron. Second Kings 23:15-20 records that before King Josiah destroys the profane shrines of Samaria, he has all the Samaritan high priests slain on their own altars. Led by King Asa of Judah, God's people covenanted in 2 Chronicles 15:12-15 to kill anyone— young or old, man or woman—who refused to worship the LORD. Exodus 22:20, Deuteronomy 13:12-18, and Zechariah 13:2-3 all prescribed the death penalty for those who worshiped other gods or prophesied in the name of a false god. Simply put, the Old Testament provided ample, and often vivid, precedent for persecution in the name of God and for the sake of religious purity. With the authority of Old Testament Scripture serving as both sanction and model, then, contemporary kings who used force against religious deviants could, with some justification, claim to be upholding the worthy tradition of Israel's biblical rulers. "Like their great predecessors," writes Coffey, Protestant kings "had a duty to purge their lands of idolatry and heresy and to establish the true religion."[9]

Baptists and other opponents of persecution did not dispute the fact that some Old Testament texts justified—and, in some cases, even demanded—persecution of religious non-conformity. In the face of clear biblical evidence, they could hardly do otherwise. Instead, they insisted that, as Christians, they did not read the Old Testament as an isolated account of God's will for the world, cut off from the further, fuller truth about God that had been revealed through the life, death, and resurrection of Jesus and the subsequent testimony of his apostles. In other words, they believed that the *Old* Testament could be properly understood only in light of the *New* Testament, with the latter serving in all cases as the most accurate standard for Christian faith and practice.

In doing so, they found themselves reading in good company. Indeed, the authors of the New Testament itself frequently took much the same Christ-centered approach—often called typological, or allegorical—to interpreting the Old Testament. The Gospel of Matthew consistently portrays events in the life of Jesus as fulfillments of Old Testament prophecy. At several points, John's Gospel describes Jesus as a successor to Moses who completes the unfinished work of salvation. Paul uses an allegorical argument about the Old Testament figures Hagar and Sarah in order to help the Galatians understand the relationship between law and grace. The entire book of Hebrews serves as an extended allegorical interpretation of Jesus in light of Old Testament practices of ritual sacrifice. As New Testament scholar Robert Grant puts it, because these early Christian writers understood the work of God as continuous and consistent—that is to say, because they believed God's essential character did not change—"they therefore regarded the events described in the Old Testament as prefigurations of events in the life of Jesus and his church."[10]

Like a fully human, fully divine Rosetta Stone, then, Jesus provided the hermeneutical key for properly interpreting all Old Testament prophecies, practices, and principles—including the punishments and persecutions doled out by the biblical rulers of Israel. Holding up the example of the ancient Hebrews as somehow normative for Christians simply did not make any sense to Baptists, for it confused God's old way of dealing with his people through the law of Moses with God's new way of dealing with them through the grace of Jesus Christ. As Leonard Busher, an early Baptist prisoner of conscience, put it in 1614, "Christ hath not only set us free from all ecclesiastical laws and ordinances, which himself hath not commanded in his last will and testament, [but also] from the ecclesiastical laws and commandments of the Old Testament."[11]

For Baptists reading Scripture from the vantage point of the New Testament looking backwards, then, religious persecution was the unfortunate—but altogether predictable result—of what John Coffey calls "a terrible hermeneutical and theological error." Old Testament Israel and its laws had only been intended as a temporary arrangement for God's people, a foreshadowing of Christ's spiritual reign over the church. "By treating Israel as a permanent model for Christians," writes Coffey, "proponents of uniformity were confusing the

Law and the Gospel and revealing their failure to comprehend the great transformation that had occurred with the coming of Christ."[12] Accordingly, Baptist writers in the seventeenth century went to great lengths to point out, and correct, this grave theological mistake.

And persecution was indeed, as early English Baptists argued again and again, a theological mistake above all else. Old Testament Israel was a unique phenomenon, they pointed out, unprecedented and unrepeatable. "The whole nation," Thomas Grantham wrote, "was consecrated to God as his church upon an act of covenant made with the seed of Abraham according to the flesh, and hereupon their church was national and the forms of their church-government and state-government were delivered by God to Moses, and by Moses to the whole nation, as the oracle of God . . . the Holy Scripture being the statute book for both."[13] The arrival of Jesus Christ into the world, however, brought an abrupt end to the Old Testament era in which God had given Israel's kings both civil and spiritual authority over his people. This combination of "high priesthood and kingly dignity, as they were typical," Grantham asserted, "ceased *de jure* when Christ had fulfilled his priesthood upon the cross and was exalted at the right hand of God to be a Prince and a Savior."[14] In place of an earthly nation bound together by blood, God had now created a new people, defined not by their biological relationship with Abraham but instead by their spiritual relationship with Jesus Christ.

Times had changed—and, these Baptists insisted, so had God's way of dealing with the world. The authority that God had once invested in the mortal rulers of Israel, he now placed in the hands of his eternal Son, Jesus, who chose to exercise that authority in a very different way. Those proponents of persecution who argued most vociferously "for a coercive power and jurisdiction" in religious matters, wrote Henry Robinson, an independent Baptist, in 1644, "do levy their main strength and forces from the Old Testament, acknowledging that what they find in the New Testament is . . . no express command or precedent of persecuting for conscience's sake."[15] Indeed, no one disputed the fact that the Old Testament kings had the power to punish religious error, wrote one group of

Baptists prisoners in 1660, "but the gospel that we live under is another dispensation, in which the Lord Jesus is the only law-giver: who doth not, as Moses, proceed against the transgressors of his precepts by external force and power, to the destroying them in their bodies and estates in this life, but in long-suffering waits on men, not willing they should perish, but rather that they should repent and be saved."[16]

Simply put, then, for English Baptists in the seventeenth century, the New Testament trumped the Old, and the life of Jesus served as the proper hermeneutical lens through which all Scripture should be understood. There is, however, one more hermeneutical shift we need to consider before proceeding further. As one group of Baptist historians and New Testament scholars has observed, Baptists have, at every point in their history, been committed "Biblicists, convinced that Scripture is the center of revelation and the guide for doctrine and practice in the church and in the individual."[17] The authority of Scripture has rarely been a matter of dispute among Baptists.

Nevertheless, the fact remains that an enormous chasm—both chronological and conceptual in nature—separates us from our seventeenth-century Baptist ancestors and the way they read the Bible. We live in what is increasingly called a "postmodern" world. The loyal dissenters of the 1600s lived in the twilight of a "premodern" world. In between these two ways of thinking stands the scientific, rational "modern" world that emerged out of the Enlightenment, or the Age of Reason, defined here as the period of Western history from, roughly, 1650 to 1800. For people who have better things to worry about, the supposed distinctions between these three worldviews—premodern, modern, and postmodern—might seem trivial or even nonsensical. After all, human nature has remained remarkably (if unfortunately) consistent ever since God cast Adam and Eve out of Eden. Could the way we think *really* have changed all that much during the same period? Well, the short answer is yes. Our frames of reference have indeed shifted, and accounting for that shift will help us better understand how our Baptist ancestors read and interpreted Scripture.

The late Baptist theologian Stanley Grenz provided a nice introduction to the world of postmodern thought in which he also helpfully described its two precursors. In the premodern era, Grenz wrote, "divine revelation functioned as the final arbiter of truth. The task of human reason, in turn, was to seek to understand the truth given through revelation."[18] In other words, premodern thinkers sought to reconcile their own experience of the world with the teachings of Scripture and the church. When conflict between the two arose, revelation always took precedence over experience. Modern thinkers, beginning roughly in the mid-seventeenth century, reversed this relationship and instead appealed "to human reason rather than externally-imposed revelation as the final arbiter of truth."[19] The modern worldview insisted that there was indeed such a thing as objective, absolute truth, and it could properly be discerned only through the rigorous exercise of reason. The scientific method, for example, with its commitment to empirical testing, precise measurements, verifiable hypotheses, and repeatable conclusions reflected modernity's singular commitment to rational authority. Consequently, other sources of authority, such as the Bible, were dismissed as unreliable superstition. A person might well be "religious," but in order to have his or her ideas taken seriously in the modern world, these ideas had to be expressed in distinctly nonreligious terms that were accessible to all rational individuals, regardless of their personal religious persuasions (if, in fact, they claimed any at all).

The conceptual break between the premodern and modern mindsets was sharp, and its implications profound, especially among Christians who take the Bible seriously. For Baptists in seventeenth-century England, the Bible represented not merely one source of authority among many. The Bible stood alone as *the* authority. From our postmodern vantage point, however, this kind of unqualified confidence in Scripture may seem a bit naïve. We tend to be instinctively suspicious of authority, in whatever guise it might assert itself. After all, wrote Grenz, the postmodern mentality "resists unified, all-encompassing, and universally valid explanations" of the universe and our place in it—in other words, the kind of explanations that the modern world insisted could be obtained through the rigorous application of human reason.[21] According to Grenz, our stubborn suspicion of authority stems from the failure of modernity to deliver on its grand promises of universal peace, progress, and prosperity. Accordingly, then, the postmodern hermeneutic might be best described as *skeptical.* Premoderns trusted revelation. Moderns trusted reason. Postmoderns, it seems, trust nothing but their own intuition, as informed by personal experience—thus the conceptual gap that confronts us when we sit down to read Scripture with the early English Baptists.

Like it or not, that gap exists. The fact that it does exist, and must be accounted for, may very well explain why contemporary Baptists are frequently more comfortable talking about religious liberty in terms of general principles derived from Scripture than in terms of Scripture itself. Biblical revelation is truth that comes to us from an external source, and, however it may be interpreted, its authority resides beyond the reader's control. General principles derived from the Bible are much more flexible and can be adjusted, adapted, and accommodated as needed. Freed from the specific context of Scripture—the holy text of a particular faith tradition—in order to be more widely applicable, their authority is largely a function of their utility. In other words, general principles can be either followed or ignored as the situation requires. They don't demand that we submit to their authority in the all-or-nothing way that biblical revelation does. Rather, in the postmodern mindset, freethinking, reasonable individuals enjoy the prerogative of determining for themselves what is (and isn't) legitimate authority. Not surprisingly, general principles inspired by Scripture are much more amenable to this intuitive understanding of authority than are actual verses of Scripture that carry their own implicit authority as the written word of God.

When reading the Bible with the early English Baptists, then, we must remember that any problem we might have with its authority is just that—*our* problem. (Once again, admitting that twenty-first-century readers may be skeptical of the Bible's authority is not at all the same thing as denying the Bible's authority. The fact that Neil Armstrong walked on the moon is not altered by the strange persistence of conspiracy theories claiming that NASA staged the whole thing.) Doubt about the Bible's authority was neither chronic nor widespread among Baptists in seventeenth-century England, and we commit the grave historical sin of anachronism if we insist that their reading of (and confidence in) Scripture be burdened with the same kind of skepticism that burdens ours.

Moreover, our willingness to take a seventeenth-century Baptist approach to the Bible—if only for the duration of this book—may encourage us to revise our own biblical hermeneutic for the better. As the late baptist (he preferred the more ecumenical implications of the lowercase *b*) theologian James McClendon observed, the distinctively "baptist" approach to Scripture

> is the way the Bible is read by those who (1) accept the plain sense of Scripture as its dominant sense and recognize their continuity with the story it tells, and who (2) acknowledge that finding the point of that story leads them to its application, and who also (3) see past and present and future linked by a . . . mystical identity binding the story now to the story then, and the story then and now to God's future yet to come.[22]

Reading the Bible alongside our early English ancestors gives us a crash course in what this sort of mystical identity looks like in practice. These faithful Baptists believed that the word of God spoke through Scripture just as clearly and immediately in the seventeenth century as it did when it was first delivered, and deserved to be taken just as seriously now as it was then. This truth, they insisted, came from God, and so, without apology, they allowed Scripture to shape their arguments for freedom of conscience and religious liberty. Perhaps by listening more closely to their voices, we can learn to do likewise.

Notes

1. Warren Carter does a nice job elaborating on this point in *Seven Events That Shaped the New Testament World* (Grand Rapids MI: Baker Books, 2013) 21ff.

2. John Coffey, *Persecution and Toleration in Protestant England, 1558–1689* (Harlow, England: Longman, 2000) 22. Coffey here provides an excellent, concise history of the Christian persecuting tradition.

3. The Donatists were Christians who believed that the validity of a sacrament such as baptism depends on the personal holiness of the one administering it. Eventually declared a heresy, this belief emerged following the Diocletian persecutions of the early fourth century, during which some church leaders compromised with the Roman authorities in order to avoid fines, prison, or worse. After the persecutions ended, those leaders who had resisted the Roman pressure (and suffered as a result) rejected the spiritual authority of those who had, for the sake of convenience, compromised. Chief among them was a bishop, Donatus Magnus, whose name became attached to the heresy.

4. Augustine's defenders insist that his words were later taken out of context to justify violence, such as torture and execution, that would have horrified the devout bishop. Augustine may have sanctioned coercive pressure, they write, but in the name of love and never through excessive force. See, for example, Henry Chadwick, "Augustine," in *Founders of Thought* (Oxford: Oxford University Press, 1991) 263–65. For more on Aquinas and persecution, see Thomas Aquinas, *Political Writings*, ed. R. W. Dyson (Cambridge: Cambridge University Press, 2002) 268–75.

5. Coffey, *Persecution and Toleration in Protestant England*, 23–24.

6. Ibid., 29–30.

7. See, for example, John Calvin, *Institutes of the Christian Religion*, ed. John T. McNeil, trans. Ford Lewis Battles (Philadelphia: Westminster Press, 1960) bk. 4, ch. 20, sec. 6ff.

8. Oliver O'Donovan has argued that the model of Christendom, in which earthly rulers bow down before the throne of Christ, can be understood as a tangible sign that God has blessed the church's witness in the world. See O'Donovan, *The Desire of the Nations: Rediscovering the Roots of Political Theology* (Cambridge: Cambridge University Press, 1996) 195ff.

9. Coffey, *Persecution and Toleration in Protestant England*, 31.

10. Robert M. Grant, *A Short History of the Interpretation of the Bible*, 2nd ed. (London: SCM Press, 1984) 37.

11. Busher, "Religion's Peace," in E. B. Underhill, *Tracts of Liberty of Conscience and Persecution, 1614–1661* (London: J. Haddon, 1846) 27.

12. Coffey, *Persecution and Toleration in Protestant England*, 62–63.

13. Thomas Grantham, *Christianismus Primitivus* (London: Francis Smith, 1678), treatise 2, bk. 3, ch. 3, sec. 1, 17.

14. Ibid., bk. 3, ch. 3, sec. 2, 18.

15. Henry Robinson, *John the Baptist, Forerunner of Jesus Christ, or A Necessity for Liberty of Conscience* (London: n.p., 1644) 79.

16. William Jeffery, George Hammon, John Reeve, and James Blackmore, "An Humble Petition and Representation," in Underhill, *Tracts of Liberty of Conscience and Persecution*, 305.

17. *The Acts of the Apostles: Four Centuries of Baptist Interpretation*, ed. Beth Allison Barr, Bill J. Leonard, Mikeal C. Parsons, and C. Douglas Weaver (Waco TX: Baylor University Press, 2009) 67.

18. Stanley Grenz, *A Primer on Postmodernism* (Grand Rapids MI: Eerdmans Publishing Company, 1996) 62.

19. Ibid.

20. Benjamin Keach, *The Baptist Catechism, or A Brief Instruction in the Principles of Christian Religion*, 16th ed. (London: John Robinson, 1764) 7.

21. Grenz, *Primer on Postmodernism*, 12. For another helpful survey of the postmodern mindset and its implications for faith-based truth claims, see Roger Lundin, *The Culture of Interpretation: Christian Faith and the Post-Modern World* (Grand Rapids MI: Eerdmans, 1993). Another good resource is Merold Westphal's *Whose Community? Which Interpretation?: Philosophical Hermeneutics for the Church* (Grand Rapids MI: Baker Books, 2009), in which the author argues that postmodernism does not necessarily mean "anything goes" relativism. Instead, he explores the ways in which a postmodern approach to reading the Bible can lead to a deeper, better understanding of the text.

22. James W. McClendon, Jr., *Doctrine: Systematic Theology*, vol. 2 (Nashville: Abingdon Press, 1994) 45.

Chapter 3

Conviction

Civil Authority Has No Power over Religion

The Baptist movement began, in part, as a struggle for freedom. This is a fair statement, as far as it goes. To contemporary ears, however, it suggests a kind of spiritual equivalent to the American Revolution, with oppressed individuals throwing off the heavy yoke of external authority and claiming the right to make their own decisions for themselves in the name of religious self-determination. It is an appealing image, with John Smyth and Thomas Helwys standing in as seventeenth-century Sons of Liberty working tirelessly—and at great personal risk to themselves—for spiritual independence. For Baptists in the United States, especially, talk about freedom instantly conjures these sorts of associations, perhaps not intentionally but rather as a matter of habit or reflex.

The truth is far more nuanced. From the beginning of their Christian witness, Baptists did indeed talk about freedom—staked their lives on it, in fact—but it was a particular *kind* of freedom that flowed from a particular way of understanding God's movement in their lives, and it circulated widely among restless Christians of all sorts in England during the 1600s. As British historian J. C. Davis notes, the "freedom to respond to God's providential promptings, to submit to his rule, and to labor in his service, these aspirations permeate the language of the puritan revolution," of which most Baptists were sympathetic, if not active, supporters.[1] Seldom, if ever, was the issue framed as a conflict between freedom and authority in the abstract, as if the two were mutually exclusive ideas. Instead, the struggle revolved around the question of where true spiritual authority lay for Christians and, moreover, how that authority could best achieve "the expression of religious freedom—not as a pluralistic or individualistic concept, but as an idea of substantial Christian dynamic."[2] In other words, the struggle for freedom in spiritual matters was not against *all* authority but rather against *wrong* authority.

Hence Baptist arguments for freedom always began by locating religious authority where they believed it rightly belonged: with Jesus Christ and Scripture, not the English monarchs and their church. "I cannot see how it should be in the power of magistrates to compel any against their will, seeing it is God, not man, that makes Christians," wrote Thomas Grantham in 1674, punctuating his observation by quoting the apostle Paul's claim in Ephesians 2:10 that "We are [God's] workmanship, created in Christ Jesus unto good works, which God hath ordained, that we should walk in them."[3] Indeed, the early Baptist conviction that civil authority has no power over religion was not intended to suggest that there was *no* authority over religion, save an individual's own conscience. Far from it. For Baptists, what was at stake in their defense of individual conscience was the freedom to submit to the *proper* authority. As Grantham put it in his multivolume work, *Christianismus Primitivus* (1678), "it is part of the Christian religion that the liberty of men's consciences should be preserved in all things, where God hath not made a limit or set a restraint." Why? The reason, Grantham explained, was so "that the soul of man should be free and acknowledge no master but Jesus Christ."[4]

Not only did Jesus exercise his spiritual authority graciously and patiently but, perhaps most important as far as Baptists were concerned, he exercised it *exclusively* as the God-ordained head of the church. This radical claim (radical, at least, in the context of a world in which the English church recognized the English monarch as its head) came directly from the New Testament Scriptures, and Baptists took it seriously—seriously enough, in fact, to make it the basis for one of their distinctive faith convictions. Where did Baptists get the idea that civil authority has no power over religion? Simply put, they got it from verses such as Ephesians 5:23, in which the apostle Paul writes that "Christ is the head of the Church, and the same is the Savior of his body," with no qualifiers or hidden strings attached, and no room for any other person or power to claim a share of that authority.

And there, of course, lay the problem, for the Church of England's structure suggested a sort of power-sharing arrangement that Baptists found both presumptuous and plainly at odds with the revealed truth of Scripture. "God forbid that any man should equalize himself with Christ, who alone is head of the church, as the husband is of the wife," wrote Baptist pastor John Murton in 1615, citing the above-mentioned verse from Ephesians. Furthermore, he added, Christ "hath left no vice-regent in that his office" to rule during the period between his ascension into heaven and his return to earth (as defenders of the established church liked to claim), "for he is never absent from his church."[5] Murton cited Jesus' assurances to his disciples in Matthew 18:20 ("For where two or three are gathered together in my Name, there am I in the midst of them.") and Matthew 28:20 (". . . and lo, I am with you always, until the end of the world.") as evidence to bolster his assertion. Scripture, Murton concluded, simply did not make allowances for anyone to sit beside Jesus—even in a subordinate role—as a spiritual authority over the church. "All that any mortal man can be, is to be a subject of [Christ's] kingdom," he wrote, with reference to James 4:12, "for there is but one Lord and one lawgiver" in all matters spiritual.[6]

The very idea of religious persecution ignored this biblical reality and presumed to place mortals in the dubious position of acting as spiritual lawgivers, brash rivals for the authority that rightfully belonged to God alone. "To force and constrain men and women's consciences to a religion against their wills is to tyrannize over the soul as well as the body," insisted Leonard Busher.[7] A king might reasonably claim to have authority over the latter. Baptists did not dispute that. In fact, as we shall later see, throughout these long years of religious persecution, they remained remarkably loyal to their earthly rulers and mindful of their duties as royal subjects. A king's claim on any aspect of the human soul, however, presented a very different challenge and, in deference to Scripture, the early Baptists recognized that an individual's soul—and, by extension, an individual's conscience—remained the exclusive domain of God Almighty, the one true Lord and spiritual lawgiver. A jealous God left no room for anyone else inside that sacred space. If the Church of England and the civil magistrates who enforced its customs did not respect this divine privilege, then they did so at their own peril. Baptists were not willing to take that risk. Indeed, wrote Roger Williams, since the coming of the Lord Jesus, they "have openly and constantly professed that no civil magistrate, no king, no Caesar, have any power over the souls or consciences of their subjects in the matters of God and the crown of Jesus."[8] To grant any mortal man or woman even the slightest share of God's authority was, as John Sturgion, a Baptist preacher, put it in 1661, "a crying sin."[9]

Moreover, it was a sin that flew directly in the face of Jesus' own testimony about himself and his disciples. Referring to Jesus' claim in John 17:16 that his disciples "are not of the world, as I am not of the world," Grantham pointedly asked "how, then, can worldly government be concerned in matters of Christian religion?"[10] All Christians, he continued, served "under Christ's authority only, held forth and exercised in the Scripture and by the Church assisted with his Holy Spirit, which is sufficient for the government of his kingdom."[11] Simply put, the King of kings did not need any additional assistance from the lesser princes of this world. It seemed to Grantham and his fellow Baptists that anyone who read the Bible should plainly be able to see the fallacy at work in the logic not only of persecution but also of *any* attempt by worldly governments to influence matters of religious faith and practice. For these Baptists, the very idea would be roughly analogous, in contemporary terms, to the North Carolina state legislature passing speed limit laws for a rural province in China. Perfectly legitimate authority in one realm may not carry any significance at all in another—and, as far as religion was concerned, Baptists found in the Bible that Jesus had both firmly and clearly limited the reach of all worldly government.

On this conviction, seventeenth-century Baptists proved doggedly consistent, even on those rare occasions when the civil authorities attempted to make their lives easier. In March 1672, for example, Charles II issued a Declaration of Indulgence, which granted dissenters in England the right to worship "according to the lights of their consciences, without restraint or disturbance, provided their teachers were licensed, their doors set open, and [they] preached no sedition."[12] During the indulgence's brief lifespan (suspecting that Charles had issued the declaration to boost the fortunes of England's Roman Catholics, a fiercely Protestant Parliament quickly and successfully pressured him to withdraw it), the crown issued 1,610 licenses for preaching outside the confines of the Church of England. Only 210 of them went to Baptists.[13] The reason for such a relatively small number? In a word: principle. Many Baptists refused even to *apply* for a license in the first place, insisting that the king had no more business granting them the right to preach the gospel than he had denying it.

Unwilling to dissent in private—because, after all, Jesus himself had plainly instructed his disciples not to hide their lights under a bushel basket—Baptists in the Lincolnshire area sent a pair of local preachers to deliver a message to the king. Thomas Grantham was one of them. After politely thanking Charles for the indulgence, the two Baptists bluntly told the king that "they thought his royal declaration infringed that liberty which as Christians they had a right to" and beseeched "him to leave them to the light of Scripture with respect to the exercise of [their] spiritual gifts."[14] In other words: Please mind your own business, your Majesty.

It was, to be sure, a rather bold thing to say to a king. Grantham understood, though, that he was speaking not on his own authority but instead on the authority of Jesus, "our Savior, who has led us the right way," by his teaching in Matthew 22:21 that it is right to "Give therefore to Caesar, the things which are Caesar's, and give unto God those things which are God's." Citing this verse from Matthew as biblical warrant, Grantham maintained that the person who "fears God will give to God the things which are God's" without exception.[15] It is true, he wrote, that Christians are to be loyal and obedient subjects of their earthly rulers. If we take Jesus' commandment seriously, then "we may hence fairly infer, that whatsoever bears the king's authority, or is required in his name, must be obeyed." Jesus' words, however, cut both ways. "Caesar's superscription is only to be put to the ordinances of man," Grantham explained. "None can put a divine character upon a law but God; and we must give to God the things which are God's, Divine Obedience, or obedience in all divine things to God, Civil Obedience, or obedience in all civil things to Caesar." Thus, he concluded, "has our Savior divided the matter of Christians (and all men's) obedience to God and to Caesar. Let us hold to this just settlement; a better cannot possibly be given."[16]

Matthew 22:21 thus clarified the vexing question of spiritual jurisdiction, with Jesus himself establishing the proper limits of Caesar's authority over his subjects. "Having given (we trust) to Caesar his due," Grantham wrote, "we may (without offense) give unto Jesus Christ the government of the church as Christian."[17] In matters of the spirit, kings could certainly issue opinions—just like anyone else—but they had no divine right to enforce them. If such a right did exist, Grantham wondered, then what things truly *could* be considered "those which are God's" and, therefore, beyond the reach of earthly powers? There is, he wrote, "a necessity that obedience in religious cases be due to God, or else He has nothing else peculiar in or over us."[18] In other words, for Jesus' teaching in Matthew 22:21 to make sense, there must be some part of our lives that, by definition, does not belong to Caesar and is the exclusive domain of God. "Since, therefore, God Almighty has reserved all religious obedience to Himself and that every man give an account of himself to God," Grantham reasoned, that sacred area must be the soul, where conscience resides and religious convictions are formed.[19]

Here, at the edge of this sacred area, the early English Baptists built their defenses against encroaching civil power—in some cases while literally at war with it. We do not know a great deal about Samuel Richardson, for example, other than the fact that he wrote a fiery tract in 1647 arguing "that religion ought to be free."[20] Historical evidence indicates that, when the English Civil War began a few years later, he became a soldier—warily at first, but soon with great enthusiasm—as well as a preacher in Oliver Cromwell's New

Model Army. Moreover, the fact that his signature appears prominently under several confessions of faith published between 1643 and 1646 by seven London Baptists congregations suggests that he was also a leader of some stature in the church during those years.[21] Challenging the king's right to assert authority where he had none, Richardson insisted that "it is God's prerogative only to force religion, by working faith in men's hearts. For though religion be natural, yet true faith is supernatural and proceeds from the Spirit of God."[22]

Give therefore to Caesar the things that are Caesar's, and give unto God those that are God's. For English Baptists in the seventeenth century, these words of Jesus from Matthew 22:21 proclaimed a limit to royal authority, placing the mystery of faith just beyond the king's grasp. Respecting this God-given and Christ-ordained constraint on civil power protected the freedom of each individual to respond, either positively or negatively, to the Spirit's movement in his or her heart. Perhaps more important, it also served as a recognition of God's sovereignty over the territory he had claimed for himself.

Nevertheless, this Baptist willingness to tolerate diverse religious opinions—including those that departed from the safely established norms of England's national church—struck some defenders of the faith as a dangerous acquiescence in the face of repeated attacks on divine sovereignty. Surely, they wrote, God-fearing Christians should not allow the Lord's holy name to be insulted by associating it with ideas, doctrines, and practices that so clearly deviated from established orthodoxy. If God rules as sovereign over all religious truth, then those who recognize his sovereignty must defend God's truth by attempting to silence those who challenge it. Simply put, what would these oh-so-tolerant Baptists do about blasphemy? The question, as Baptists themselves acknowledged, was a reasonable one and deserved a response. Henry Danvers, for one, addressed the issue in a tract written, interestingly enough, in 1649—at least a year before he was baptized.[23] How did Baptists answer their critics who accused them of promoting blasphemy? Affirming God's exclusive sovereignty over all matters of faith, Danvers wrote that insofar as blasphemy is concerned, "the offense is to God, who alone 'gives judgment against all men, and rebukes all the ungodly among them of all their wicked deeds, which they have ungodly committed, and of all their cruel speaking, which wicked sinners have spoken against Him' (Jude 15), who may, if it seems good in his sight, cut them off, as he did Ananias and Sapphira. Or what if he please to magnify his patience and long suffering on them, though vessels of wrath, it is for his praise."[24] In other words, as a sin against God, blasphemy was not the king's problem. It represented, instead, a breach of faith to be dealt with by the proper authority, whom the book of Jude identifies as none other than the Lord.

John Murton had written much the same thing a generation earlier. He recognized the reality of blasphemy and religious error, for the early English Baptist passion for freedom did not exclude their equally passionate conviction that there was such a thing as divine truth. Some opinions about the nature of Christian faith and practice were wrong. Those who hold errors and refuse to obey the truth do indeed sin against God and will be punished, Murton maintained, but *God* will do the punishing at a time of *God's* own choosing.[25] As biblical warrant for this position, he pointed to three specific Scripture references: Romans 2:8-9, Mark 16:16, 2 Thessalonians 1:8. Again, for Baptists, the primary question was not "Should blasphemy be punished?" but rather "Who has the legitimate authority to punish blasphemy?" As Baptists read the New Testament, there was little ambiguity as to the correct answer. "You think you do God good service in burning Christians that differ from your religion," wrote Leonard Busher in 1614, but Scripture tells a different story, insofar as the power to destroy false believers and confirm true believers "belongeth to God alone. And therefore," Busher concluded, citing John 6:44, "Christ saith 'No one can come to me unless drawn by the Father who sent me; and I will raise that person up on the last day.'"[26]

When early English Baptists read their Bibles, what they found there convinced them that the coming of Jesus Christ had fundamentally changed the relationship between civil power and religion. The Old Testament example of ancient Israel, in which kings bore a God-given responsibility to punish religious error through coercive and sometimes even violent measures, no longer served as a model for Christian rulers to follow. False teaching, blasphemy, heresy, and assorted other tragic failures to believe, understand, and practice the truth of God's word would no doubt persist into the future. It was indeed possible for people to be wrong about religion. The witness of Scripture, however, persuaded early English Baptists that, with the coming of Jesus into this world, authority over spiritual matters had been transferred entirely over to God. The power over religion that the Lord once invested in Israel's kings to be exercised by the sword, he now placed completely in the hands of his Son to exercise through the Spirit. In obedience to Matthew 22:21, Baptists willingly gave Caesar his due in all matters over which he properly held sway—but they also understood these words of Jesus to mean that the soul belonged to God, and over it no civil power held any authority whatsoever, either to bless or to punish.

Reading Matthew 22:21 Together

When English Baptists in the seventeenth century read Matthew 22:21, they heard Jesus establishing a limit on the authority of civil power. Caesar did have legitimate concerns in this world—collecting taxes, for example—and, in those areas, he could exercise his power as he saw fit. Not everything, however, was subject to Caesar's coercive rule. Some things belonged to God alone, and over them, civil power could claim no rightful authority. While Baptist writers cited numerous verses of Scripture in support of their faith conviction that civil power had no authority over religion, Matthew 22:21 was a frequent and favorite citation. In other words, when early English Baptists wanted to argue that spiritual matters were beyond the scope of legitimate human authority, they often turned to the words of Jesus as recorded in this verse for support. So, as fellow readers of Scripture, let's take a closer look at this verse from Matthew that helped our Baptist ancestors articulate what they believed to be true about the proper relationship between civil power and religion.

In order for us to get a better understanding of the specific verse in question, we need to realize that it is but one small part of a long-simmering controversy between Jesus and the Jewish authorities in Matthew's Gospel, an already heated situation well on its way to boiling by the time we get to chapter 22. According to Matthew's timeline, the day after Jesus triumphantly enters Jerusalem, the chief priests and elders question his authority at the temple (Matt 21:23-27). Jesus responds to their challenge with three very pointed parables (21:28–22:14), all of them casting the Jewish leaders in a decidedly negative light. After Jesus' third parable, Matthew tells us that "then went the Pharisees and took counsel how they might entangle him in talk" (22:15). They have finally heard enough from Jesus and are ready to take the necessary measures to shut him up. In fact, the conversation about taxes that begins at Matthew 22:1 is the first of three attempts by religious authorities (a tit-for-tat response to Jesus' three parables?) to embarrass Jesus with a controversial question. Demonstrating that, even in biblical times, politics makes for strange bedfellows, the Pharisees, who were zealous keepers of the Mosaic law and wary of Rome's influence, form a convenient alliance here with the Herodians, a Jewish party known for being cozy with the pagan Roman government. And what is the glue holding this unlikely coalition together? A shared contempt for Jesus.

So the Pharisees send their disciples, along with their new Herodian friends, to see Jesus. The emissaries begin their mission with a burst of flattery that is more revealing than they intend. Every bit of praise thrown at Jesus—"Master," they call him, praising his integrity and his skill as a true teacher of God's way (Matt 22:16)—boomerangs on these smooth talkers, who have repeatedly shown themselves to be insincere teachers of a distorted view of God's truth, adept primarily at demanding deference and delivering judgment. Their flattering description of Jesus, ironically, spells out exactly what these pharisaical ambassadors are *not*.

Their flattery having quickly run its course, these *agents provocateurs* get to the point. "Tell us, therefore, how thinkest thou," they demand, maneuvering Jesus into an uncomfortable corner. "Is it lawful to give tribute unto Caesar, or not?" (Matt 22:17) The law to which they are referring here is not that of Rome but rather the commandments of God as found in the Torah, meaning that their question is about the *religious* propriety of paying tax to Rome, specifically the annual property tax that the Romans collected from those living under their imperial rule. (The New Testament Greek word translated here as "tribute" is khnsoz, or *kensos*, from which the English word *census* comes. In order to tax property, the Romans first had to account for it.) Taxes are rarely popular in any time or place, but for Jews (Herodians possibly excepted) chafing under the rule of Rome, this yearly tribute to Caesar aroused particular resentment. The tax not only supported the Roman army that occupied Jerusalem but also had to be paid in Roman currency—that is, with coins bearing an image of the pagan emperor, Tiberius, underneath the grandiose (and, to the Jews, blasphemous) title, "Son of the Divine Augustus." Cleverly presented to Jesus as a referendum on the religious implications of paying tribute to Caesar with profane currency, the question puts Jesus in an awkward position: he must either *condemn* the tax as inconsistent with Jewish law and, in doing so, attract the potentially dangerous attention of Rome—or he must *endorse* the unpopular tax and earn the contempt of the crowd. That, at least, is how his interrogators have planned it.

Instead, Jesus avoids the trap set before him by choosing neither option. Aware both of the malicious game afoot and its potentially-high stakes (Matthew 22:18), Jesus asks to see a Roman coin, which his inquisitors quickly produce (Matthew 22:19). This detail, by the way, suggests that, while Jesus didn't carry any Roman money, his holier-than-thou opponents—disciples of the Pharisees, no less—did. No wonder Jesus calls them hypocrites![27] After having first established that the emperor's head and the emperor's title are indeed on the coin (Matt 22:20-21a), Jesus delivers to the gathered crowd his artful response: "Give therefore to Caesar the things which are Caesar's, and give unto God, those which are God's" (22:21b). Matthew tells us that Jesus' answer stuns his opponents, who wander off amazed (22:22).

Like many of Jesus' difficult teachings, this one challenges much more than it comforts. Indeed, anyone relying on Matthew 22:21 to systematize the messy process of sorting out the competing claims of God and Caesar will find it a frustrating formula, to say the least. Jesus never actually tells us what rightfully belongs to whom, nor does he set down any guidelines to help us make these distinctions for ourselves. Had he done so, it is doubtful that the crowd would have walked away marveling at his answer. They would have called him either a traitor (for endorsing the Roman tax) or a fool (for opposing it in public). Rather, the genius—and the uncomfortable challenge—of Jesus' answer lies with the fact that it stirs up more questions than it settles. We want a neat, paint-by-numbers approach to negotiating our priorities: *this* belongs to Caesar, *that* belongs to God, and so forth. By this point in Matthew's Gospel, however, we should know better than to expect such a thing from Jesus. He doesn't negotiate priorities. Instead, he sets them.

In Matthew 6:24, for example, Jesus speaks about conflicted loyalties—in this instance, the conflict between our desire to serve God and our desire to make money—in very straightforward terms. "No man can serve two masters," he says. "For either he shall hate the one and love the other, or else he shall lean to one and despise the other. You cannot serve God and riches." Jesus does not pretend that there is a golden mean between the two, or a way somehow to divide our lives in such a way that allows us to serve both masters faithfully at the same time, but in different ways. The same goes for family ties and all the other close relationships we enjoy in this world. "He that loveth father or mother more than me is not worthy of me," Jesus teaches his disciples in Matthew 10:37. "And he that loveth son or daughter more than me is not worthy of me." Jesus is not dispensing advice here about finding balance. He's instructing his disciples to put him first in their lives. He must be their priority.

So, by the time we get to Matthew 22, Jesus has established a precedent. His disciples will have to make choices in this world. To whom will they be loyal? Who (or what) will they serve? To what end will they devote their lives? Will they serve God, follow Jesus, and pursue the kingdom of heaven above all else? These are not rhetorical questions. As followers of Jesus in every time and place have discovered, there are always plenty of other options, and no shortage of other, lesser gods to stake claims on our devotion. In chapter 6, Jesus calls attention to the power of money as a potential master. In chapter 10, he acknowledges the power of family as a potential rival. Now, in chapter 22, in response to the apprentice Pharisees and their Herodian allies, Jesus considers yet another potential source of conflict, this time in connection with the power of Caesar and the demands he makes on the lives of those under his rule.

While his nimble response to the question posed in Matthew 22:17 is, by necessity, more of an *ad lib* answer than a carefully crafted opinion, Jesus' position in chapter 22 is consistent with what he said in chapters 6 and 10. At first hearing, Jesus' admonition to give "Caesar the things which are Caesar's, and give unto God, those which are God's" sounds an awful lot like he's endorsing the very kind of divided loyalty he has previously rejected: you can't serve both God and money, and there isn't a happy medium between your love for family and your love for me—but it *is*, in fact, possible to work out a compromise between your loyalties to God and Caesar. A closer listen, however, suggests that he is actually doing just the opposite. The belief that all creation—everything in heaven, on the earth, and under the earth—belongs to God was a fundamental article of faith for Jesus and his fellow Jews. As Psalm 24:1 puts it, "The earth is the LORD's, and all that therein is; the world and they that dwell therein."

With this in mind, then, Jesus' response to the Pharisees' disciples and the Herodians takes on a much more confrontational tone, posing a challenge to anyone tempted to compromise their convictions at Caesar's convenience: What, in all of creation, could there possibly be that doesn't *already* rightfully belong to God? The answer, of course, is "Nothing." It *all* belongs to God, to be used in accordance with God's will. Just as money and family are both capable of serving noble purposes and, as such, do have their respective places in the lives of Jesus' disciples, the same is true for the power of Caesar. At no point, though, can Caesar (or the king, or the government, or any other civil power in this world) lay an exclusive claim on anything—our bodies, our souls, our resources, or our allegiance—to do with as he pleases, because none of it truly belongs to him. This doesn't mean, however, that Caesar won't try. The powers of this world—money and family included—will always try. And when that happens, when what Caesar asks of us conflicts with what God expects from us, then Christians must be prepared to choose accordingly and live with the consequences of those choices.

This reading of Matthew 22:21, however, seems to put us at odds with our early English Baptist ancestors. They understood these words of Jesus as establishing a boundary between the legitimate, worldly concerns of Caesar (such as, for example, taxes, armies, and the necessity of establishing and maintaining public order) and the spiritual domain where God alone exercised sovereignty. The king, these Baptists argued, had no right to interfere with religion because the human soul and its affections were beyond his jurisdiction. Spiritual matters, in other words, fell into the Christ-given category of "those [things] which are God's" and, therefore, were none of the king's business. Our reading of Matthew 22:21 rejects this compartmentalized understanding of the world—with God and Caesar each enjoying the right to do what they will on their own turf—in favor of the view that all creation (including the powers of this world) belongs to God and is subject to his divine command. There is no such thing as Caesar's turf and God's turf, with a fence neatly separating the two. Rather, any claims that Caesar makes on the lives and loyalties of Jesus' disciples are legitimate only insofar as they are consistent with what God has revealed to us of his will through the written record of Scripture and the living example of Jesus.

The apparent tension here between these two interpretations of Matthew 22:21 could reflect more of a difference in degree than a true difference in kind. In reading, and then proclaiming, these words of Jesus as they did, our Baptist ancestors in the seventeenth century discovered in Scripture the sliver of daylight they needed in order to advance the radical argument that there were some things—or, rather, there was at least *one* thing—in England over which the king had no authority. The king could tax his subjects, force them to fight his wars, and throw them in prison for disturbing the peace, but he could not dictate to them either what they should believe about God or how they should put those beliefs into practice. With Matthew 22:21 as a guide, Baptists reasoned that, if anything rightly belonged to God, it was a person's soul. As such, religious opinion was a matter of individual conscience and beyond the king's authority to control. Royal power, in other words, did have its limits.

It was a bold argument to make in seventeenth-century England, bold enough to put many Baptists on the wrong side of the law and in the king's jails. It was also a necessary first step in the direction of bolder, even more radical arguments that Baptists would later make for religious liberty and the institutional separation of church and state. We can read Matthew 22:21 today as a declaration of God's sovereignty over all creation (including the pretensions of Caesar's descendants) precisely because the early English Baptists understood Jesus to be saying that there was, in fact, a limit to Caesar's authority in the first place. As philosopher Alasdair MacIntyre has suggested, "a tradition is an argument extended through time."[28] When Baptists today speak about our traditional conviction that civil power has no authority over religion, we are simply extending an argument that began, in part, with Matthew 22:21. Therein lies the gift of reading Scripture together, even across the centuries.

Hearing Matthew 22:21 Together

The congregation at Murfreesboro Baptist Church in Murfreesboro, North Carolina, heard the following sermon on Sunday, 11 October 2011.

What Belongs to God?
Matthew 22:15-22

About a month ago, on September 23, scientists at Europe's main physics laboratory in Switzerland made a startling discovery. Maybe you heard about it. The scientists were shooting subatomic particles called neutrinos through the earth's crust to an underground sensor located under a mountain 450 miles away. The surprise was that these neutrinos arrived at their destination 60 billionths of a second faster than it would have taken for light to travel that same distance. Sixty billionths of a second? Doesn't sound like much, but in the world of subatomic nuclear physics, though, that tiny fraction of the blink of an eye could very well represent the beginning of the end of the world as we know it—or, at least, the world as we can *explain* it.

You see, I don't understand Albert Einstein's famous formula, $E=mc^2$, but it makes me feel better to know that there are some people who do understand it, some people who can take this equation and use it to make sense out of this complicated universe in which we live. What makes these 60 billionths of a second so potentially disruptive, though, is that, according to Einstein's theory of special relativity, nothing can travel faster than the speed of light. Go faster than the speed of light, and time moves backwards. In theory, that's impossible. But, if those neutrinos in Switzerland did, in fact, travel faster than the speed of light, then everything we thought we knew for sure about the scientific universe might well turn out to be incomplete and insufficient. In short, we suddenly face a situation in which we have no formulas or equations or neatly packaged scientific laws to explain everything there is to explain in the physical world around us.

Now, unless you're a subatomic nuclear physicist, this possibility has probably not caused you any sleepless nights. I know that my life has not been noticeably affected by the discovery of super-speedy neutrinos. But I will confess that when I first heard the news, it did make me go *hmm*. Another layer of uncertainty, another unpredictable variable. One more thing we can't account for. One more thing that's not nailed down. One more thing that feels beyond our control. This is the stuff anxiety is made of, and so, whenever we can, we take comfort in formulas, in rules of thumb that help us make sense of the world and figure out how best to maneuver our way through it. They help clarify matters and reduce complex situations down to more manageable proportions. Either you're with us or you're against us. Go for the tie at home, go for the win on the road. Buy low, sell high. Feed a cold, starve a fever. Or is it starve a cold, feed a fever? I never can remember. Anyway, a good rule of thumb is always a welcome traveling companion when trying to negotiate a complicated world.

That's why, I think, we Christians—Baptists, especially—have made so much out of Jesus' words in Matthew 22, verse 21: "Give therefore to the emperor the things that are the emperor's, and to

God the things that are God's." Now *there*, it seems, is a formula we can use: a rule of thumb to help us negotiate the competing claims of church and state, a nifty yardstick to help us figure out what to do when the sacred and secular are at odds and we're stuck in the middle between the two. Give Caesar what belongs to Caesar. Give God what belongs to God. It's quick. It's simple. It's convenient. And it's frequently used to justify the compartmentalization of our lives: this part belongs to God, the rest is for me and Caesar to enjoy. There's Sunday, and there's the rest of the week—and as long as we give God a couple of hours or so on the Lord's day, then we're pretty much free to do as we please on the other six days, as long as Caesar doesn't object.

The thing is, though, I don't believe that's what Jesus meant when he said these words in verse 21. When it comes to God's claim on our time, our money, our heart, soul, mind, and body, Jesus—throughout the Gospels—never in any way advocates compartmentalizing our lives, or separating them along the lines of God and Caesar, sacred and secular. For Jesus, there is no such thing as divided loyalty. It's all or nothing.

So let's take a look at what's going on here in Matthew 22. The exchange with the Herodians and the Pharisees-in-training that begins at verse 15 is actually the first of four consecutive attempts by Jewish leaders to publicly embarrass and discredit Jesus that Matthew tells us about in this chapter. Boom! Boom! Boom! Boom! It's like theological dodgeball, with Jesus in the middle surrounded by a bunch of guys throwing high, hard heat. Now, as you may remember, in dodgeball you don't plan your moves ahead of time: *Hmm. First, I'll hop to the left, then fake back to my right . . .* No, in dodgeball you instinctively react to where the ball goes. The only formula for success in dodgeball is *Don't get hit*. So jumping first *this* way, then *that* way, Jesus is doing his best to stay on his feet against a determined bunch of adversaries while still, at the same time, speaking the truth about God.

That's what's going on here. Matthew tells us right off the bat that this is no friendly exchange of ideas. Verse 15: "Then the Pharisees went and plotted to entrap Jesus in what he said." And, to do the trapping, the Pharisees first send out the junior varsity—some of their students plus a group of Jews loyal to King Herod, the local ruler installed and supported by the Romans. So these guys go to Jesus and butter him up a little with some flattery. Then they take their shot: "Tell us, then, what you think. Is it lawful to pay taxes to the emperor or not?"

Now, as "gotcha" questions go, this one's pretty transparent—but it's also pretty crafty. Is it lawful to pay taxes to the emperor or not? We can imagine the crowd's interest perking up, ears straining forward to hear how Jesus will answer. If he says *Yes*, then his fellow Jews are liable to attack him as a compromising sell-out to Rome, whose soldiers occupy Israel. If Jesus says *No*, then the Romans can arrest him as a dangerous political agitator. It's a classic lose-lose proposition.

They may only be the JV, but these Herodians and Pharisees-in-training could hardly do a better job putting Jesus in a tight spot. They've asked him whether it's lawful to pay taxes to the emperor—and by "lawful" here, they mean "morally just according to Jewish law." In other words, it's a religious question, not a matter of politics or economics. They've asked Jesus whether it's morally right in the eyes of God to pay taxes to the hated Romans. So Jesus asks for one of the coins used to pay the imperial tax. Someone in this little band of interrogators digs around in his pocket and produces a denarius. Pointing to the Roman coin, Jesus asks them, "Whose head is this? Whose title is this?" The emperor's, they answer.

Suddenly, the tables turn. It's as though Jesus has picked up the dodgeball and thrown it right back at them. Who's going around carrying Caesar's money? It's not Jesus. It's the very people who've been trying to paint Jesus into a corner as a compromiser and a sell-out to the Romans. They're the ones who have the Roman money on hand. They're the ones who carry the graven image of Tiberius Caesar in their pockets. They're the ones who've clearly bought into the pagan economic system in which money makes the world go round. Their hypocrisy is now on display for everyone to see. And, so Jesus drives his point home: you Pharisees and Herodians know the law. You know what God expects of you. You also know what the emperor wants from you. "Give therefore to the emperor the things that are the emperor's and to God the things that are God's."

Jesus isn't talking compartmentalization here. He's not talking some here, some there. He's talking *either* here *or* there—but not both. You see, just about everyone involved in this conversation, either as a participant or a spectator, most likely would have been familiar with Psalm 24, which tells us that "the earth is the LORD's, and all that is in it; the world and all who live in it." In other words, everything belongs to God. It's a basic article of Jewish faith: Everything belongs to God. So in verse 21, what Jesus is really doing is challenging his listeners to make a choice, to declare themselves one way or another: Will you give God what belongs to God—that is, your whole heart, soul, mind, and strength—*or* will you give those things to someone else?

As far as Jesus is concerned, there is no such thing as divided loyalty. We've heard him say this before in Matthew's Gospel, back in chapter 6: no one can serve two masters, for a slave will either hate the one and love the other, or be devoted to the one and despise the other. In chapter 6, Jesus is talking about God and mammon: you can't serve both. Now here, in chapter 22, he's talking about God and Caesar, and the message is the same: You can't serve both. Our lives, our values, our priorities—the things we think are important, the factors that influence our decisions—they're going to be shaped one way or another. The question is, who will do the shaping? Will it be God and his ways of justice and righteousness, or will it be Caesar and his ways of blood and money?

Jesus does not offer an ironclad rule or a convenient formula for portioning out our obligations and resolving the inevitable tensions that arise between God and the secular powers of this world. Most of us wish he had given us that kind of yardstick. The peer pressures, the subtle coercions, the persistent nudges that this world brings to bear in order to influence our decisions and define our loyalties: we deal with them each and every day, and so it's no wonder, then, that we eagerly latch onto verse 21 as a neat and tidy rule of thumb for determining how and for whom we should spend our lives. Give the emperor what's his and give God what's his. Sounds simple, but we all know that, in practice, this rule of thumb ends up being yet one more way for us to rationalize giving the powers of this world what we know rightfully belongs to God. Whenever we try to make these neat divisions between what's sacred and what's secular, let's be honest: whether it's time, money, loyalty, whatever—who almost always ends up with a bigger share of whatever's at stake?

Rather than simplifying matters and making them more *manageable*, Jesus here actually makes them a lot more complicated for us. After all, how are we going to give God our whole selves—heart, mind, body, soul—while living in a world that demands those very same things of us? As a Christian, for example, my body belongs to God—and yet, when I turned 18, I was legally bound to register for the draft, which put my body at the disposal of Caesar. As a Christian, everything I have is a gift from God to be used for his glory—and yet, every April 15, I am legally bound to turn over a chunk of it to Caesar. Romans 13 tells us to obey the emperor. Revelation 13 encourages the saints to resist unjust rulers and suffer the consequences. It can get complicated, no doubt about it. Neither God nor the powers of this world recognize the artificial boundaries we construct to separate the sacred from the secular in our lives. To God, it's all sacred. To Caesar, it's all secular. So which master will we serve? To whom will we give our lives?

We want from Jesus some firm lines of demarcation. What we get from Jesus is a reminder that we owe God what belongs to God—which is, really, everything: all we have, all we are, all we ever hope to be. It all belongs to God and is at God's disposal—and, once we claim Jesus as Lord and give ourselves to God, then God's priorities, God's interests, God's desires become the only standards that matter if we want to get through this world with our faith and our integrity intact. And what are God's priorities and interests and desires? Read through the Old Testament prophets. God's priorities show up in just about every verse: justice, righteousness, generosity, obedience, peacemaking. Who we're serving determines how we'll serve—and, if we get the who right, then the how becomes a bit clearer. Not any easier, mind you, but at least clearer.

When it comes to making our way through this world and discerning the legitimate claims that Caesar—or any of the secular powers-that-be—might make on us from those claims that demand too much of us, well, the truth is, there is no neat formula that always works in every situation. Instead, it's a lot more like dodgeball: the way we move will depend on how the questions, the issues, the challenges come at us. Sometimes we'll go this way, sometimes we'll go that way. Sometimes we'll do well just to stay on our feet while speaking God's truth. How we move will vary, where we move will vary, but why we move will not change. Why do we make the commitments we make? Why do we live in *this* way and not in *that* way? Why? Because we belong to God. That's why. After we've given God what's rightfully his, then, if there's anything leftover, well, the world can have it. Chances are, though, there won't be any leftovers—and that, brothers and sisters, is what salvation looks like. In the blessed name of Jesus, amen.

Living in Light of What We Have Read Together

In his book *Soft Power: The Means to Success in World Politics* (2005), Joseph S. Nye, Jr., distinguishes what he calls "soft power" from the more traditional, or "hard," ways that nations exercise power on the world stage.[29] Nye knows what he's talking about. He is the former dean of the Kennedy School of Government and served as an assistant secretary of defense in the Clinton administration. Hard power, he writes, flexes steel-toned muscles of guns, tanks, missiles, aircraft carriers, and drones. It also speaks the language of economic sanctions and trade embargoes. Hard power is coercive, and tries to achieve its objectives by bending an adversary's will through the use of force. Hard power seeks to subdue enemies. Soft power, conversely, tries to make friends. It is cooperative and collaborative, and encourages others to participate in the process of achieving objectives that seem mutually beneficial to everyone involved. Nations that exercise soft power successfully make other countries want to work with them. Dropping cluster bombs, for example, is an exercise in hard power. Hosting the Olympics, meanwhile, is soft power in action. The

Marine Corps? Hard power. The Peace Corps? Soft power. Manipulating the exchange rate? Hard power. Welcoming exchange students? Soft power.

Nye's observations from the arena of international relations can teach us something about the temptations we face as Christians seeking to be faithful followers of Jesus in a world where things are not always as they seem. Along with our early English Baptist brothers and sisters, we believe that civil power has no authority over—or, for that matter, any business being involved in—religion. In the United States, the practical implications of this Baptist faith conviction have even been incorporated into the American framework of government via the First Amendment to the Constitution. While there are countless court cases each year devoted to hashing out where the various legal boundaries separating God and Caesar ought to lie, the principle that civil power has no authority over religion is no longer a matter for serious debate in this country. The days of Caesar taking the hard power approach of imposing fines, beatings, and jail time for the purpose of coercing religious conformity are long gone. That's a good thing, and Baptists deserve a large share of the credit for it.

The happy decline of *hard* power, however, doesn't mean that there is *no* power at Caesar's disposal to use in his age-old conflict with God over who will enjoy the lion's share of our allegiance. The *soft* power of Caesar is insidious, seductive, and stakes claims on us that we often don't recognize as posing a threat to the integrity of our Christian witness. Prayers at official government functions, flags in sanctuaries, religious displays on public property—these and so many other examples of God and Caesar sharing public space all seem so well-intentioned and essentially harmless that it's difficult (and often awkward) to argue against them. Why would a Christian object to opening city council meetings with a prayer for God to guide our elected officials in their work? Why would a patriotic American have a problem with displaying our nation's flag? What could possibly be wrong with a local church setting up a crèche in front of town hall at Christmas as a way of reminding people about the reason for the season? At first (and even second or third) glance, none of these activities appear to be particularly dangerous, or corrosive, to a robust public expression of the Christian faith. In fact, if anything, they seem to reflect a friendly, healthy working relationship between God and Caesar in which the values of one both support and reinforce those of the other.

Such is the subtle effectiveness of soft power in action, persuading committed Christians to allow—and sometimes even invite—civil authority into religious territory where Baptists once believed Caesar had no business going. Our early English spiritual ancestors believed that, as the living body of Christ, consisting of baptized believers united by a freely professed faith in Jesus as their Lord and Savior, the church served as the one, true witness to the truth about God and the gospel of salvation. It was the church's unique responsibility to share this good news with the world, for it was through the church alone that God had chosen to continue the work of Jesus. The king, meanwhile, had his own affairs to attend to, none of which properly concerned religious matters or questions of individual conscience. To allow—or, worse, to invite—the king, or his officials, to exercise any influence over the content, context, or purpose of Christian prayer, for example, would have been unthinkable. (Remember, these were people who refused to apply for preaching licenses because they refused to concede that the king had any right to license preaching in the first place!) The king had no business in the church, and the church had no business, either literally or figuratively, in the halls of government.

When religious liberty, however, is written into the law of the land, as it is in the United States, soft power can serve as Caesar's most effective means of expanding his territory. Every time we participate in, or advocate for, government-sponsored prayers, we compromise boundaries that the early Baptists sought to fortify. Every time we display national flags in sacred spaces of worship, we compromise boundaries that the early Baptists sought to fortify. Every time we request permission from the government to put religious displays on public property, we compromise boundaries that the early Baptists sought to fortify. The fact that we aggressively pursue these compromises (and others like them) with such enthusiasm—and castigate as anti-Christian and un-American anyone who questions their propriety—suggests just how thoroughly susceptible we are to the seductions of soft power. We make Caesar's job a lot easier when we are willing agents of our own domestication.

So how can our Baptist ancestors from the seventeenth century help us to keep Caesar in his place today—or, at the very least, help us to stop inviting him to make himself at home where he doesn't belong? Legal arguments against blurring the lines between church and state may be sound enough, and compelling enough, to win court cases and persuade lawmakers to protect religious liberty. Appealing to the First Amendment in defense of a religious conviction, however, is not the same thing as offering a full-throated, faith-based account of why Baptists believe as we do that civil authority has no power over religion. After all, atheists and dedicated opponents of religion also make strong arguments for their cause by appealing to the First Amendment. A distinctively *Christian* witness about the limits of civil authority—one capable of proclaiming our faith convictions to nonbelievers while, at the same time, convincing our fellow believers to leave Caesar to his own devices—is best built on a distinctively Christian foundation, and for that our Baptist ancestors confidently turned to the New Testament.

In Scripture, they found ancient voices that could be trusted to tell them the truth about God, Caesar, and what each could rightfully demand from an individual. In Scripture, they discovered that there were indeed limits to a king's authority—and, at the same time, no limit to God's sovereignty. They turned to the Bible and, in verses such as Matthew 22:21, they heard Jesus tell them to be careful about what they gave to whom, for under no circumstances should a Christian offer to Caesar what properly belongs to God. We do well to remember their example of how to talk faithfully about the limits of civil authority in matters of religion and conscience, using the language of Scripture as both inspiration and justification. We can, in other words, articulate our beliefs about God and Caesar in a way that not only says something about where we stand but also says a great deal about who we are. It's been done before. The early English Baptists have shown us how to begin to do so again.

Notes

1. J. C. Davis, "Religion and the Struggle for Freedom in the English Revolution," *The Historical Journal* 35 (1992): 528.

2. Ibid., 529.

3. Thomas Grantham, *The Loyal Baptist, or An Apology for the Baptized Believers* (London: Thomas Fabian, 1674) 38.

4. Grantham, *Christianismus Primitivus*, (London: Francis Smith, 1678) treatise 2, bk. 3, ch. 3, sec. 3, 22.

5. John Murton, "Persecution for Religion Judged and Condemned," in E. B. Underhill, *Tracts of Liberty of Conscience and Persecution, 1614–1661* (London: J. Haddon, 1846) 109.

6. Ibid. James 4:12 reads, "There is one Law giver, which is able to save, and to destroy. Who art thou who judgest another man?"

7. Busher, "Religion's Peace," in Underhill, *Tracts of Liberty*, 35.

8. Roger Williams, *The Bloudy Tenent of Persecution* (1644), ed. E. B. Underhill (London: The Hanserd Knollys Society, 1848) 49.

9. John Sturgion, *A Plea for Toleration of Opinions and Persuasions in Matters of Religion* (London: S. Dover, for Francis Smith, 1661) 16.

10. Grantham, *Christianismus Primitivus*, treatise 2, bk. 3, ch. 3, sec. 2, 19.

11. Ibid.

12. Thomas Crosby, *The History of the English Baptists*, vol. 3 (London: John Robinson et al., 1740) 82.

13. Michael R. Watts, *The Dissenters: From the Reformation to the French Revolution* (Oxford: Clarendon Press, 1978) 248.

14. Crosby, *History of the English Baptists*, 3:82–83.

15. Grantham, *Loyal Baptist*, 23.

16. Ibid., 34.

17. Grantham, *Christianismus Primitivus*, treatise 2, bk. 3, ch. 3, sec. 2, 19.

18. Grantham, *Loyal Baptist*, 23.

19. Ibid.

20. Samuel Richardson, "The Necessity of Toleration in Matters of Religion" (1647), in Underhill, *Tracts of Liberty*, 253.

21. W. A. Shaw, rev. Sean Kelsey, "Samuel Richardson," *The Oxford Dictionary of National Biography*, ed. H. C. G. Matthew and Brian Harrison, vol. 46 (Oxford: Oxford University Press, 2004) 845.

22. Richardson, "The Necessity of Toleration," 253.

23. Richard L. Greaves, "Henry Danvers," *The Oxford Dictionary of National Biography*, ed. H. C. G. Matthew and Brian Harrison, vol. 15 (Oxford: Oxford University Press, 2004) 100. Danvers was baptized while serving as governor at Stafford, in northern England, where he won praise for organizing troops against invaders from Scotland. Later, Danvers became involved in a number of plots and conspiracies, including one to assassinate Charles II and restore England as a republic. Eventually, he made his way to the Netherlands, where he died in 1687.

24. Henry Danvers, *Certain Quaeries Concerning Liberty of Conscience* (London: Giles Calvert, 1649) 4.

25. Murton, "Persecution for Religion Judged and Condemned," in Underhill, *Tracts of Liberty*, 118.

26. Busher, "Religion's Peace," in Underhill, *Tracts of Liberty*, 78.

27. I am indebted to Thomas Long for suggesting this creative angle on the coin's significance. See Long, *Matthew* (Louisville KY: Westminster John Knox Press, 1997) 250–52.

28. Alasdair MacIntyre, *Whose Justice? Which Rationality?* (Notre Dame IN: University of Notre Dame Press, 1988) 12.

29. See Joseph S. Nye, Jr., *Soft Power: The Means to Success in World Politics* (Jackson TN: Public Affairs, 2005).

Chapter 4

Conviction

Persecution on Account of Religion Is Wrong

When Charles II, promising "liberty to tender consciences," returned to England in the spring of 1660, he assured his soon-to-be subjects that none of them would ever "be disquieted, or called into question, for differences of opinion in matters of religion which do not disturb the general peace of the kingdom."[1] At first, Baptists and other religious dissenters in the kingdom responded to this royal guarantee of toleration with cautious optimism, despite the persistence of sometimes-violent local opposition. Not long after Charles's return, for example, a mob disrupted worship services at William Kiffin's Baptist church in London. Other dissenting congregations faced similar harassment.[2] Unfortunately, the king's seemingly ironclad assurances of toleration soon proved to be rather elastic, particularly where "the general peace of the kingdom" was at stake. Governments in the twenty-first century can usually find ways to stretch the definition of "national security" far enough to justify measures that limit their citizens' freedoms. In seventeenth-century England, "the general peace of the kingdom" served the same purpose, giving Charles II a convenient excuse for taking repressive measures against non-conformists—which he did almost immediately after the religiously inspired Fifth Monarchist uprising fizzled in January 1661. An emergency decree from the king on 10 January 1661 severely limited the freedom of religious dissenters to assemble; Parliament later incorporated this royal decree into a series of laws, known collectively as the Conventicle Acts, aimed at preventing traitors from meeting together for devious purposes under the pretense of engaging in non-conformist worship.

Among the English Baptists who protested this crackdown on religious dissent was John Sturgion, a pastor in Reading. Not long after the emergency order went into effect, Sturgion published an open letter to Charles II, reminding the king of his earlier promise to protect liberty of conscience. Threats of violent insurrection and treason, Sturgion admitted, could not safely be ignored; the king and Parliament did indeed have a responsibility to protect the peace. Nevertheless, he continued, non-conformists who had initially trusted the king's assurances now found themselves in an untenable situation, "whereby the Innocent suffer for the Guilty; and many of Your Majesty's loyal and obedient subjects are questioned, and publicly suspected to their great prejudice in their reputations."[3] Restricting religious freedom in an effort to stamp out political dissent, Sturgion argued, not only punished the wrong people but also had the ironic effect of turning honest subjects into dishonest suspects. A person who attempts such coercion injures "a man for keeping a good conscience or forces him into a bad; he both punishes sincerity and persuades hypocrisy; he persecutes truth and drives into error; [and] he teaches a man to dissemble, to be safe, but never to be honest or acceptable to God."[4] A person might say anything in order to escape a fine, a prison term, a beating, or worse. *Saying* something, however, is not the same thing as *believing* it.

As a matter of *principle*, Sturgion and his fellow English Baptists were firmly convinced that persecution on account of religion was wrong. They formed this conviction based on their reading of Scripture, particularly the words and deeds of Jesus himself. We will, in due course, take a closer look at some of these New Testament texts. But first, it's worth noting that, as a *practical* matter, the early Baptists consistently argued that coercion in matters of conscience simply did not work—*if* its purpose was, in fact, to redirect hearts, minds, and spirits away from error and toward truth. As far as Sturgion and his fellow advocates of toleration were concerned, the evidence supplied by common sense and human nature pointed to the same verdict:

persecution just didn't work. To a large extent, writes historian John Coffey, this conclusion flowed logically from a general belief among tolerationists that, because genuine faith "could only be produced in the conscience by persuasion and the work of God's Spirit, it was futile to try and coerce it."[5] To put it in rather simplistic terms, people can't believe what they can't believe, and so punishing them for their failure to believe accomplishes nothing that's good and much that's evil. Anyone who uses "force upon the body to change the mind, or to make men believe something they are not persuaded of, or to disbelieve something they have received for truth, or to leave off worshipping God in that way which they think is most agreeable to His will," wrote Sturgion, "will have no better success than that man who clapped his shoulder to the ground to stop the earthquake."[6]

Moreover, insisted Thomas Grantham, given the fact that different kings in different nations practiced such very different religions, the idea of equating the king's religion with the true worship of God defied logic. Do all kings everywhere—"some heathen, some Turkish, some popish"—engage in the true worship of God when they worship in their own fashion? Grantham answered his own rhetorical question with an emphatic *no*.[7] Prominent Baptists Thomas Monck, Joseph Wright, George Hammon, William Jeffrey, Francis Stanley, William Reynolds, and Francis Smith echoed this point in a joint petition to the king dated 8 May 1661, and written "in hopes of stemming the violence that is affecting us all."[8] If civil magistrates in England have the power to coerce religious belief, they argued, then all magistrates in all nations must enjoy the same authority, meaning that, "as the authority changes religion, we must do the same—but God forbid, because nothing is more absurd!"[9] Another petition to the king, this one written a year earlier from a prison in Maidstone by a group of Baptist preachers that included the aforementioned Jeffrey and Hammon, offered a thought experiment to illustrate this absurdity. Imagine, they wrote, that a king converts to Christianity in a nation where only 5 percent of the people are Christians. By the logic of persecution, those who aren't Christians—fully 95 percent of the population—could rightfully be destroyed if they refused to convert to the king's faith. Because such an outcome "cannot possibly be supposed to be warrantable," the logic of persecution falls apart under its own weight.[10] Common sense alone suggested that religious coercion didn't work.

Moreover, Baptists argued that the weak and capricious reality of human nature also tended to undermine the case for persecution. When individuals are punished for their religious beliefs, wrote Leonard Busher, they usually don't *change* their beliefs. Instead, they *conceal* them. Everyone keeps his own conscience while outwardly conforming, he observed, with the result being that "all the church is a confused Babel, full of every unclean and hateful bird, even a hold of foul spirits."[11] Coercive measures aimed at purifying religious faith and practice thus have the unintended consequence of forcing dissenting opinions to burrow deeper under protective cover. When that happens, false beliefs can't be corrected, even by the gentler means of patient instruction or persuasion, because those who hold them refuse to voice them for fear of punishment.

Other Baptists pointed out that the very real possibility of human error presented further complications for those who advocated coercion. It's important to remember, insisted one group of dissenters in a letter written from prison, that the magistrates of this world are mortal and not infallible. After all, they pointed out, Pontius Pilate, the Roman government's duly appointed civil authority, put Jesus to death for being an enemy of Caesar.[12] If an imperial Roman governor could make such a tragic error in judgment regarding the Son of God, then how much greater are the risks for ordinary individuals whose fate rests in the hands of ordinary magistrates? The Maidstone prisoners advanced a similar argument. "Consider that neither thyself nor councillors have the spirit of infallibility," they wrote. "It is possible many of those that are accounted false worshippers and heretics on this day may, at the time when God shall judge the world in righteousness, be found the servants of the Most High God."[13]

Busher couldn't resist pointing out the ironic fact that, when it came to tolerating dissenters, the Muslim rulers of the Ottoman Empire had a much more generous record than the current Christian king of England. "I read that Jews, Christians, and Turks are tolerated in Constantinople, and yet are peaceable, though so contrary one to the other," he wrote in 1614. "If this be so, how much more ought Christians not to force one another to religion?" Written in all capital letters, Busher's concluding words leapt off the page with a blistering ferocity: "AND HOW MUCH MORE OUGHT CHRISTIANS TO TOLERATE CHRISTIANS WHEN AS [sic] THE TURKS DO TOLERATE THEM? SHALL WE BE LESS MERCIFUL THAN THE TURKS?"[14]

Such appeals to reason placed seventeenth-century English Baptists in the company of other advocates for toleration who were making similar arguments in those days, such as John Milton and Henry Robinson.[15] The overwhelming burden of the Baptist case against religious persecution, however, rested not on common sense or the limitations of human nature. Instead, when these Baptists articulated their conviction that persecution on account of religion is wrong, Scripture served as their primary language—in particular, the life and teachings of Jesus. Persecution was contrary to the essential nature of the gospel, wrote Sturgion. "It would be a mighty disparagement" to the good news of Jesus, he continued, "that in its principle it should be so merciful and humane, and in the promotion and propagation of it, so inhumane and dishonorable to Christ."[16] Persecution, the early Baptists believed, compromised the integrity of the Christian witness. Violent, coercive actions did not honor the Prince of Peace, nor did they further his cause. Instead, when Baptists read the New Testament, they discovered that Jesus himself had already established a precedent for dealing with unbelievers.

"The whole New Testament throughout, in all the doctrines and practices of Christ and his disciples, teach no such thing as compelling men by persecutions and afflictions to obey the gospel, but the direct contrary," declared John Murton in 1615. "To suffer at the hands of the wicked; when they were persecuted for righteousness sake, to suffer it; when the unbelievers and wicked curse them, to bless them and pray for their repentance and that God would forgive them and never lay these sins to their charge, as our Savior, Stephen, and the rest did."[17] Busher took a similar position, interweaving biblical references into the course of his argument as was frequently done in those days. As an example of this early English Baptist style, it's worth quoting Busher at length:

> Christ's kingdom is not of this world, therefore it may not be purchased nor defended with the weapons of this world, but by his word and Spirit (Ephesians 6:10, 17). No other weapons will be given to his church, which is his spiritual kingdom. Therefore, Christ saith, "He that will not vouchsafe to hear thee, tell it unto the Church: and if he refuse to hear the Church also, let him be unto thee as an heathen man, and a Publican" (Matthew 18:17). He saith not burn, banish, or imprison him; that is anti-Christ's ordinance. And, though a man be a heretic, yet ought he not to be burnt but to be rejected, "after once or twice admonition" (Titus 3:10)—that is, cast out of the church.[18]

Jesus neither compelled others to follow him nor authorized his followers to exercise any dominion over the faith of others. "And, in truth," observed the Baptists in Maidstone jail, "the apostles and disciples were not to use any external force to carry on their master's work, but only by showing the terrors of the Lord, were to persuade men. And, in the case of resistance, to shake the dust from their feet as a witness against their oppresors."[19]

Jesus refused to persecute those who rejected him and his teachings. He also refused to allow his disciples to persecute those who rejected him and his teachings. As one group of Baptist dissenters pointed out, Jesus certainly had the power to persecute others if he had so desired, for, as he declared to his disciples in Matthew 28:18, "all power is given unto me in heaven, and in earth." Presumably, they reasoned, "all power" included the power to persecute others on account of their religion. Just as Jesus did not claim this power for himself or his followers, nowhere in the New Testament is there any suggestion that he delegated it to any worldly authority. If he had, they wrote, then Peter and John would certainly have behaved more submissively when hauled before the Jewish authorities in Acts 4. Instead, they refused to obey the order "to forbear that which they judged part of the worship of God, and said, 'Whether it be right in the sight of God, to obey you rather than God, judge ye. For we cannot but speak the things which we have seen and heard' (Acts 4:19-20)."[20] For these early Baptists, the New Testament precedent could hardly be clearer: persuasion, not persecution—conversion, not coercion—is the way of Jesus in this world.

Among the various, and copious, New Testament texts that helped shape this faith conviction, two proved particularly popular in English Baptist literature of the seventeenth century: Luke 9:54-56 and Matthew 13:24-30, 36-43. In the Luke passage, Jesus sends messengers ahead of him to Samaria, with instructions to make preparations for his arrival there. The Samaritans, however, refuse to welcome Jesus. When James and John hear about this rejection, they ask Jesus if he would like them to call down fire from heaven to destroy these inhospitable Samaritans. (Let's just stop for a moment and admire the sheer chutzpah of these disciples. They think they're doing Jesus a favor. Do they really believe that they have the power to call down fire from heaven?) Jesus, however, "turned about, and rebuked them, and said, 'Ye know not of what Spirit ye are. For the Son of Man is not come to destroy men's lives but to save them.' Then they went to another town" (Luke 9:55-56).

The Baptists in the Maidstone jail, for example, held up Jesus' restraint here as indicative of his overall approach to unbelievers. Neither "the Lord Jesus himself, nor his disciples, would [ever] by any outward force compel men to receive them or their doctrine," they observed. "For when the disciples of Christ, supposing they might use violence as under the law, would have commanded fire to come down from heaven, as [Elijah] did, to consume them that would not receive them, Christ turned and rebuked them."[21] At issue here for these Baptists wasn't so much the question of judgment—that is, whether those who reject Jesus will someday be judged, and subsequently punished, for their lack of faith. As a rule, early English Baptists maintained a robust confidence in the certainty of hell as the eternal destination for people who died rejecting Christ.[22] The Samaritans in Luke 9, for example, would indeed be judged for their negative response to Jesus. Few Baptists seriously questioned that. For them, rather, what Luke 9:54-56 demonstrated was Jesus' flat refusal to render—or to allow his followers to render—this-worldly judgments on matters of religious opinion. As the authors of "Sion's Groans for Her Distressed" put it, "most remarkable doth it appear that it is not the intent of the Lord Jesus that judgment should be executed on those who reject his words, to the punishing them *in their bodies and estates in this life under the law.*"[23] When Jesus had the chance to punish the Samaritans for their erroneous religious beliefs, he declined. This was the powerful lesson that early Baptists took away from Luke 9:54-56.

Far and away the most common passage of Scripture cited by seventeenth-century Baptists in their arguments against persecution, however, was Matthew 13:24-30, 36-43—Jesus' parable of the wheat and the tares. In the parable, recorded in Matthew 13:24-30, Jesus compares the kingdom of heaven to a man who sows good seed in his field only to find that, during the night, an enemy snuck into the field and sowed weeds. The planter's servants ask permission to go into the fields to pluck up these weeds, but the planter counsels patience, afraid that, in the process of removing the weeds, they might uproot some of the good, fruit-bearing plants by mistake because the wheat and tares look almost identical.[24] Wait, he tells he servants, until the harvest comes. Then the weeds can be bundled up to be burned, while the grain is safely gathered and put away in the storehouse. Several verses later, in Matthew 13:36-43, the disciples ask Jesus to explain the parable, which he does, equating the sower with the Son of Man, the good seed with the sons of the kingdom, the weeds with the sons of evil, the mysterious midnight sower with the devil, the reapers with God's angels, and the harvest with the end of time. When the end comes, Jesus tells his disciples, the Son of Man will send his angels to gather up all sinners and law-breakers and throw them in the fiery furnace. The righteous, meanwhile, will shine like the sun in the kingdom of heaven.

This parable resonated strongly with the early Baptists, who understood it to be a clear example of Jesus' remarkably patient attitude regarding the persistent presence of religious error in this world. When proponents of coercion argued that deviations from orthodoxy must always be uprooted swiftly and forcefully lest they spread, Baptists responded by pointing to the story of the wheat and the tares. In fact, when the General Baptists gathered in London to craft a standard confession of faith in 1660, their statement on liberty of conscience included just two Scripture references: the Golden Rule of Matthew 7:12, and this parable of the wheat and the tares. Persecution on account of religion, these Baptists wrote, "we confidently believe is expressly contrary to the mind of Christ, who requires that whatsoever men would that others should do unto them, they should even so do unto others, and that the Tares and the Wheat should grow together in field (which is the world) until the harvest (which is the end of the world)."[25]

Roger Williams, for one, made great use of this parable in his arguments against religious coercion. "Christ commandeth that the tares and the wheat, which some understand are those who walk in the truth and those who walk in lies, should be let alone in the world and not plucked up until the harvest, which is the end of the world," he wrote in his sweeping manifesto, *The Bloudy Tenent of Persecution* (1644), which was inspired, in part, by John Murton's writings from several decades earlier.[26] Only briefly a Baptist, but always a champion of a free and unfettered conscience, Williams believed that there would indeed be a time to separate truth from lies, good from evil, blessed from cursed. The power, however, to make these distinctions—and assign rewards and punishments accordingly—rested exclusively in the hands of God, to be exercised at a time of God's own choosing. In other words, when Jesus commanded patience in Matthew 13, he was endorsing neither religious indifference (i.e., it doesn't really matter) nor religious relativism (i.e., all faiths more or less lead to the same general truth, but in different ways). Williams, writes historian William Lamont, "had no illusions about human capacities, nor did [he] question a dispensation which divided mankind into two sorts of people (i.e., wheat and tares): Freedom was not an ideal to pursue, because the task of any government was to police the depraved instincts of the majority." What Williams found offensive about the practice of religious persecution, Lamont continues, "was not philosophical, but tactical. The wheat *must* be separated from the tares, but not yet." For Williams, and those who shared his confidence that the time for the final, divine harvest was near, "the imminence of that heavenly discrimination was their supreme comfort. Surrogate earthly claims were gratuitous and, in the final analysis, blasphemous."[27]

Later in *The Bloudy Tenent*, Williams offered a more detailed interpretation of the parable. Contrary to those who argued that Jesus intended the field to represent the church, a narrow reading of the parable which would render everyone *outside* the church—meaning, at least in England, all dissenters from the Church of England—fair game for persecution, Williams insisted that the field represented "properly the world, the civil state, or the commonwealth." The tares, then, "here intended by the Lord Jesus are anti-Christian idolators, opposite to the good seed of the kingdom, true Christians." So, in Williams's reading of the parable, Jesus recognizes the reality of religious diversity in this world: not everyone will believe the truth about God, and not everyone will accept Jesus as Lord and Savior. When the time comes, God alone will decide the fate of these unbelieving "tares." Williams's interpretation, though, led to what is, perhaps, a surprising conclusion. The tares should be spared not only from persecution at the hands of religious and civil authorities, Williams argued, but also from evangelistic efforts to turn them into wheat. "The ministers and messengers of the Lord Jesus ought to let them alone to live in the world," he wrote, "and neither seek by prayer or prophesy to pluck them up before the harvest."[28] For Williams, any attempt to change a person's religious convictions was tantamount to coercion and, thus, violated the liberty of conscience.

Even among liberty-loving seventeenth-century Baptists, Williams's interpretation of the parable was an outlier. Of greater concern to them—and, they believed, to Jesus—was the very real danger that religious persecution could short-circuit any possibility of conversion. In the parable, the sower forbids his servants to separate the wheat from the tares—saving the former and burning the latter—prematurely. Writing from prison in 1620 on smuggled paper and using milk instead of ink (the words would become visible again once the paper was lightly scorched), John Murton observed that the reason for the sower's patience seems to be because they who are now tares may hereafter become wheat; they who are now blind may hereafter see; they that now resist him may hereafter receive him; they that are now in the devil's power in adverseness to the truth, may hereafter come to repentance; they that are now blasphemers and persecutors, as Paul was, may in time become as faithful as he; they that are now idolators, as the Corinthians were may hereafter become true worshippers as they; they that are now no people of God, nor under mercy as the saints sometimes were may hereafter become the people of God and obtain mercy as they.[29]

Others echoed this concern. The authors of "Sion's Groans" pointed out that persecution not only made criminals out of potential Christians but also did so with a necessarily limited amount of insight. Even the wisest human authorities can be wrong when it comes to matters of religion, which is why "Jesus himself . . . forbids any outward force or violence to be exercised upon false worshippers or heretics as such."[30] He knew better than to trust fallible humans with the extremely delicate, discerning work of harvesting the field. "The tares must be those who err in worship of God," they wrote, yet they should "not be plucked up, but tolerated in the field of the world until the harvest shall come at the end of the world, when the angels, who [are] to be the reapers and infallibly can distinguish between the tares and the wheat, *which no magistrate now can*, shall gather the tares."[31]

The Baptists in the Maidstone jail argued much the same point in their appeal to the king. "It is very plain that the Lord Jesus himself," they wrote, "forbids any force to be exercised upon false worshippers as such. . . . But those that Christ Jesus would have remain amongst his wheat in the field of the world are the children of the wicked through idolatry and will-worship." Emphasizing the divine authority of their position, the imprisoned pastors then instructed the king to compare verses 28 through 30 with verses 38 and 39 of Matthew 13, thus implying that if the king would consult the Bible, he might see for himself that "the reason the Lord Jesus gives why both wheat and tares must grow together—O, King, that it were engraven with the point of a diamond and often laid before thee—is, lest in gathering up the tares, the wheat also be rooted up with them."³² How tragic it is, they continued, "to remember how in all ages since Christ, very strange mistakes have been on this account," how those supposed to be tares were killed, stoned, and even crucified when they were, in fact, "the precious wheat of God."³³

When these English Baptists read Matthew 13, they found a clear, Christ-given injunction to leave the hard—not to mention eternally significant—work of distinguishing between wheat and tares to those truly able to recognize the difference: the angels of God, acting with divine authority and under divine supervision. They understood, however, why well-intentioned Christians might feel the need to exercise worldly power in order to keep the holy field of the Lord free of what they perceived to be unsightly and potentially invasive weeds. Indeed, in most cases, Baptist dissenters charitably ascribed noble motives to those who advocated and encouraged religious coercion. "Doubtless these holy men, emperors, and bishops" who have persecuted people for reasons of conscience throughout the centuries "intended and aimed right to exalt Christ," wrote Williams, but good intentions can nevertheless result in disaster if not properly guided by biblical authority. "Not attending to the command of Christ Jesus to permit the tares to grow in the field of the world," he continued, "they make the garden of the church and the field of the world to be all one, and might not only sometimes in their zealous mistakes persecute good wheat instead of tares, but also pluck up thousands of those precious stalks by commotions and combustions about religion."³⁴

Arguments against persecution on account of religion circulated rather freely in seventeenth-century England. Those making the case for toleration could cite numerous reasons, both practical and philosophical, why coercion was not only a bad idea but also an ineffective policy—if, of course, the goal of coercion was to turn heretics and pagans into orthodox believers. For the early English Baptists, though, the most compelling argument against coercion was perhaps the simplest: it's wrong because Scripture tells us it's wrong. That's what Baptists found when they opened their Bibles and studied the example of Jesus. In obedience, then, to the word of God and the teachings of Jesus, Baptists bravely rejected the notion that persecuting others because of their religious beliefs was unfortunate but grimly necessary holy work. In reading passages such as Matthew 13:24-30, 36-43, they discovered in Jesus himself not only a model of patience and generosity worth emulating but also the humility to confess that only God could render judgment on the spiritual condition of his creatures with any sort of accuracy or legitimate authority.

Reading Matthew 13:24-30, 36-43 Together

When English Baptists in the seventeenth century read Matthew 13:24-30, 36-40, they understood Jesus to be laying down a fundamental truth about the kingdom of heaven: because only God can rightly judge who is good and evil in his sight, earthly authorities have no business persecuting people for their religious opinions and practices. The parable of the wheat and the tares, they believed, called for patience, tolerance, humility, and a willingness to trust God's judgment. Just as every plant in the field must be allowed to grow freely and unmolested until harvest time, every person must be allowed to obey the dictates of his or her own conscience in all matters pertaining to faith. These Baptists, however, could hardly be considered religious relativists of the sort who insist that all faith convictions are more or less the same, ultimately flowing from the same divine source and eventually leading to the same divine destination. In matters of religious opinion and practice, there were indeed distinct differences between good and evil, right and wrong, truth and error—after all, wheat and weeds are not at all identical species of plants. Jesus himself refused to pretend otherwise.

So, when English Baptists in the seventeenth century came to this parable, they walked away from it convinced that there *will* be a reckoning, there *will* be a sorting out, there *will* be a verdict rendered on the lives we lead and the faith we profess, but the responsibility for this judgment rests solely in the hands of God, to be done in his time and according to his will. In other words, when these Baptists considered what Jesus had to say about the wheat and the weeds, they heard one message loud and clear: "Live and let live"—at least on *this* side of Judgment Day. On the authority of this Christ-given command, then, they argued against religious coercion and in favor of religious toleration. As fellow Baptists, and as fellow readers of Scripture, let's now take a closer look at the verses from Matthew 13 that once helped our spiritual ancestors articulate their faith conviction that persecution on account of religion is wrong.

It's worth noting that this specific parable of the wheat and the weeds is one in a cluster of parables and stories, located about midway through Matthew's Gospel, that address the same general question: Who is a true follower of Jesus? In Matthew 12:24, the Pharisees account for Jesus' proficiency in casting out demons by accusing him of being in league with Beelzebub, ruler of the demons. Jesus' response—that is, Beelzebul would not take sides against his own demons, so anyone who casts out demons must be working *against* Beelzebul—leads him to issue this declaration: "Whoever is not with me is against me, and whoever does not gather with me scatters" (Matt 12:30). Several verses later, Jesus observes that, just as "a tree is known by its fruit" (12:33), so the content of a person's heart is revealed by his or her words: "The good person brings good things out of a good treasure, and the evil person brings evil things out of an evil treasure. I tell you, on the day of judgment, you will have to give an account for every careless word you utter; for by your words you will be justified, and by your words you will be condemned" (12:35-37). Finally, at the end of chapter 12, Jesus declares that "whoever does the will of my Father in heaven is my brother and sister and mother" (12:50).

Even before we get to the parables in Matthew 13, then, we hear Jesus making clear distinctions between the people of this world: those who are with him, those who are against him; those who gather, those who scatter; those who bear good fruit, those who bear evil fruit; those who do the will of his Father, those who don't do the will of his Father. Clearly, Jesus isn't promoting some mushy, I'm-okay/you're-okay, religious ethic here. As he declares earlier, in Matthew 10:34, he has come into this world with a sword to create a great division. Some will hear Jesus' message about the kingdom of heaven and follow him, while others will hear Jesus' message about the kingdom of heaven and reject him. The two responses are in no way commensurate, representing just two equally acceptable sides of the same coin, two different paths up the same mountain of divine enlightenment. There are, in other words, right and wrong answers to the questions of faith that Jesus poses: Are you with me? Will you follow me? Do you love me?

Chapter 13 begins in a similar vein, with Jesus telling (Matt 13:1-9), and then explaining (13:18-23), a parable about a sower who sows seeds that fall on different types of terrain—some favorable for growth, some not. According to Jesus' explanation of the parable, not everyone who hears his message about the kingdom will understand it and bear the good fruit of obedient discipleship. The reasons for this failure vary, but the point is clear: some people will hear what Jesus has to say and yet, nevertheless, their hearing will still not result in an enduring, vital faith. Jesus is under no illusion here about the stubborn fact of religious diversity in the world. He knows that, unfortunately, his invitation to faithful discipleship is not the only game in town. The kingdom of heaven has rivals here on earth.

A reasonable question, then, might be, how does Jesus *respond* to this diversity? How does he *deal* with the fact that not everyone who hears his gospel will accept it as truth? Perhaps more important, for our purposes, how does Jesus intend for his *disciples* to respond to such religious diversity? At this point in Matthew, it's clear that Jesus makes a distinction between right and wrong responses to his message—and, presumably, he expects his disciples not only to accept his authority to make these distinctions but also to accept that these distinctions are valid. Simply put, not everyone is this world will be a follower of Christ, so how should those who *do* follow Christ treat those who don't? As if to answer that question, in Matthew 13:24-30, Jesus puts before his disciples another parable, also agricultural in nature and concerned about what happens after the good seeds of faith are sown.

As recounted above, the parable itself is pretty straightforward. After a man sows good wheat seeds in his field, an enemy sneaks into the field under cover of darkness and sows weeds among the wheat. When the plants grow to maturity, the difference between the two varieties becomes easy to spot: some show themselves to be wheat by virtue of the grain they bear, others show themselves to be weeds by their obvious lack of grain (Matt 13:26). The man's servants come to him, shocked to discover these invasive weeds sprouting up in what's supposed to be a pristine field of fertile, fruitful wheat. Their first questions to their master are revealing: "Did you not sow good seed in your field? Where, then, did these weeds come from?" (13:27) Their question is about intent. Did the master *intend* for weeds to grow among the wheat in his field? If not, then how did these weeds get there? The master's answer indicates that he didn't, in fact, want the weeds—*and* he's well aware of how they got there: an enemy, someone bent on sabotaging the wheat crop, scattered bad seeds throughout the entire field.

The servants' next question serves as the pivot point of the entire parable. Having heard that these weeds are the result of an enemy's destructive plot against their master, the servants logically and dutifully conclude that the proper course of action is for them to make a thorough sweep of the field, removing any and all plants they find there that aren't wheat. Their question, in Matthew 13:28, sounds rather rhetorical in nature, as though they assume that they've correctly anticipated their master's wishes (as good servants are trained to do) and are now simply asking for permission to proceed—permission that they expect will be swiftly and gratefully granted: "Then do you want us to go and gather [the weeds]?" The servants are proposing to do what *anyone* who's ever tried to maintain a small garden, much less a field of wheat, would do given the same circumstances. When a gardener spots a weed, the intuitive response is to pull it up. Getting rid of weeds increases the likelihood that the good plants, the desired crop, will flourish, because there will be less competition for the precious resources of sunlight, water, and nutrients in the soil. Moreover, there will also be more room for the good plants to grow without fear of getting entangled in, and choked by, all those pernicious weeds. Anyone with any experience trying to cultivate plants knows that, *of course,* the master will want his servants to go out into the fields and get rid of all the weeds. The servants, it seems, hardly need to ask the master's permission to do such an obvious, necessary chore. Yet, because they are servants, they do work at their master's behest.

Nearly all of Jesus' parables contain a twist that reveals the peculiar logic of God's kingdom. What we think should happen in the story doesn't happen, resulting in a jarring, head-on collision between our expectations and the parable's reality. That collision then tells us something about the strange way God has chosen to work in this world. In this parable of the wheat and the weeds, it's the master's reply in Matthew 13:29-30 that provides the dramatic twist. The servants have proposed a sensible solution to the problem of the weeds. They're following conventional wisdom. The master, however, takes a very different approach. *Don't* pull up the weeds, he tells his servants, "for in gathering the weeds you would uproot some of the wheat along with them. Let both of them grow together until the harvest; and at the harvest, I will tell the reapers, Collect the weeds first and bind them in bundles to be burned, but gather the wheat into the barn." The master's plan is the exact opposite of what common sense dictates. It runs contrary to what the servants—and we, as Matthew's readers—assume would be the correct, responsible, and prudent course of action. It's not hard to imagine what the servants' protests might sound like: Won't the weeds compromise the health of the wheat? Won't the weeds take over the field? Won't the weeds diminish the quality of the harvest? These are reasonable protests.

The master, however, doesn't seem at all concerned about any negative effects that the weeds might have on the wheat as they grow together. It appears as though, in his judgment, the wheat will be plenty strong enough to flourish in the field, despite the fact that it must share both space and resources with all these invasive weeds. If the wheat is left alone, the master is confident that it will be fine. Instead, his only worry is that the wheat he so carefully sowed *won't* be left alone. His well-intentioned, just-trying-to-be-helpful servants, determined to eradicate the unwanted weeds introduced into the field by an unseen enemy, might carelessly end up destroying some good wheat in the process. Protecting the wheat is the master's priority, and if that means letting weeds grow free and unmolested in his field, then so be it. It's worth noting here that at no point in the parable does the master indicate any sympathy, or concern, for the weeds. When harvest time arrives, he fully intends for these weeds to be collected, bundled, and burned. The fact that he refuses to allow his servants to pull any weeds up before the harvest, then, shouldn't be interpreted as a sign that he necessarily welcomes, or even accepts, the presence of weeds in his field. Rather, it's a measure of the master's devotion to his crop of wheat that he's willing to tolerate the weeds for as long as he does—much to the dismay, we can only presume, of his eager servants.

On the heels of Jesus' repeated acknowledgments in Matthew 12 and 13 that the gospel will face opposition, his message will be rejected, and not every tree will bear good fruit, the parable of the wheat and the weeds sounds very much like an effort on Jesus' part to teach his disciples how to deal with those who, in the spirit of Matthew 12:30, are indeed against him. Given this context, it's fairly intuitive to assume that the wheat in the parable stands for those who accept Jesus, and the weeds stand for those who reject him. Matthew, however, wants to make sure we get it right. Like the parable of the sower, the story of the wheat and weeds conveys a lesson that is evidently too important to be left open-ended and subject to erroneous interpretation. So, in Matthew 13:36, we're told that the disciples approach Jesus, asking him to explain the parable to them. He obliges, thus confirming what we initially suspected: "The good seed are the children of the kingdom; the weeds are the children of the evil one" (13:38). At the end of the age—that is, when God is finally ready to fulfill his redemptive will for creation—Jesus declares that "the Son of Man will send his angels, and they will collect out of his kingdom all causes for sin and all evildoers, and they will throw them into the furnace of fire, where there will be weeping and gnashing of teeth. Then the righteous shall shine like the sun in the kingdom of their Father" (13:41-43a).

Because Jesus offers no additional explanation for the master's decision to let the weeds continue growing until harvest, we can only conclude here that the Son of Man's patience with evildoers is motivated by the same concern for the children of the kingdom that the master in the parable feels toward his wheat. Rather than risk the potential destruction of even one of those who belong to him, he's willing to tolerate—for a while, at least—the continued presence of sin and evil in the world. He knows that the time for harvest will come, and when it does, he plans to assign the delicate task of distinguishing wheat from weeds to those reapers who are qualified to do this sort of work. *Angels* will do the reaping, *angels* will separate children of the kingdom from children of evil, *angels* will execute the Son of Man's judgment on what he finds in this world. Nowhere in Jesus' explanation do we hear anything about the master's servants who played such a prominent role in the parable. They don't figure into this end-of-the-age harvest scene at all. In fact, if we want to make an argument from silence, we can conclude that, when it comes to the work of deciding who's in and who's out of God's kingdom, the best thing for servants of Christ to do is . . . nothing. Let the *angels* handle this delicate task. They know what they're doing. The rest of us have no clue. Jesus then punctuates his explanation with these words of added emphasis, which also sound strangely like words of warning to those disciples who might be tempted to think of themselves as potential gardeners: "Let anyone with ears listen!" (Matt 13:43b)

When the early English Baptists used their ears and listened to these words of Jesus, what they heard was a lesson about the danger of presumption in matters of religious judgment: fallible humans mustn't take it upon themselves to make the kind of careful distinctions between true and false believers that only God has the ability and wisdom to authorize. It bears repeating here that the reason for such humility was not that these Baptists rejected the idea of divine judgment. They took Jesus seriously when he indicated that, come harvest time, the weeds would all be gathered, bundled, and thrown into the fire. Nothing about Jesus' parable suggested to them that unbelievers would be spared God's judgment. Instead, the parable warned against a temptation that Jesus must have known would bedevil servants of the master time and again as they encountered in the world people who did not share their faith—namely, the temptation to act in a coercive fashion, with good intentions and sincere ignorance, against those they considered to be enemies of Jesus and his kingdom. Pulling up a weed might feel like a great service to the master, but according to Jesus, it was, in fact, directly contrary to the master's wishes. Being a good servant, instead, meant trusting the master's judgment and learning to live with the stubborn reality of weeds.

Of course, as people who were used to dealing with threats of persecution on account of their faith, the early Baptists would have been particularly receptive to these words of Jesus advocating patience and tolerance. After all, Baptists were considered to be weeds by the religious establishment in seventeenth-century England, and the parable of the wheat and the weeds comes—in the short run, at least—with a weed-friendly moral. Still, though, the Baptist conviction that coercion on account of religion runs contrary to the will and example of Jesus was not conjured out of thin air. It came from Scripture and was grounded in the words of Christ himself, which means that it retains its authority even as circumstances change.

What are the implications, then, of this faith conviction for Baptists who live in a culture where they *aren't* considered "weeds" by the religious powers-that-be? What happens when Baptists help shape that culture, when they are, in a *de facto* sense, among the religious powers-that-be? Do these words of Jesus sound different to Baptists who are now in a position to think of themselves as duly deputized servants of the master, charged with guarding the integrity of the field against invasive weeds? The conviction is no less true in the twenty-first century than it was in the seventeenth: religious persecution is wrong. Only *God* is in a position to judge the state of someone's soul, distinguish wheat from weeds, and reward or punish as appropriate. The rest of us have to learn to *get along* with one another even if we don't *agree* with one another. English Baptists in the 1600s could passionately proclaim this faith conviction with . . . well, *conviction* because they understood from their own experience what it was like to be on the business end of religious coercion. The challenge for the spiritual descendants of these Baptists who listened to Jesus four hundred years ago and took his teaching to heart is this: remaining faithful to the generous precedent established by Jesus when we may no longer be convinced that it's in our best interests.

Hearing Matthew 13:24-30, 36-43 Together

The congregation at Murfreesboro Baptist Church in Murfreesboro, North Carolina, heard the following sermon on Sunday, 17 July 2005.

The Patient Farmer
Matthew 13:24-30, 36-43

When I was a kid, one of the chores I really hated was pulling up weeds in the yard. My mom would send me out to pick weeds and I'd try to get out of doing it. I wouldn't just come right out and say no and refuse to do it. Instead, I'd take the route of passive resistance. I'd go out to the flowerbed, look it over, then come back inside and say, "You know, there's a lot of different things growing out there. How do I know which ones are weeds?"

"Just look at them," my mom would say. "You can tell which ones are weeds and which ones aren't. It's not hard."

I'd go out, pull up a few, then come back in. "Mom, I need a judgment call here. There's a big one that I *think* is a weed, but it has a flower on it. Come tell me if you want me to pull it up. I'd hate to pull up a good plant by accident." This would go on for a while until, finally, my mom would get so outdone with me that she'd just tell me to stay outside and not bother her about those weeds anymore.

Despite my attempts to act ignorant, it really wasn't too hard to distinguish between what was a weed and what was a good plant. Most folks, I think, can tell the difference. And maybe that's what makes the parable Jesus tells in our Gospel lesson from Matthew such an uncomfortable one to hear.

This is the first of several parables about the kingdom of heaven that Jesus tells in chapter 13 of Matthew. A great crowd has gathered around Jesus, eager to hear what he has to say—probably as much out of curiosity as anything else. Instead of saying something clear and straightforward to these folks, though, Jesus rewards their curiosity with a series of strange stories, beginning with a parable. "You want to know what the kingdom of heaven is like?" says Jesus. "Well, it *could* be compared to someone who planted wheat in a field. One night someone came and scattered weeds all over the field. After a while, both the wheat and the weeds started to grow and the servants out in the fields noticed something was wrong. They asked their Master if he wanted them to pull up the weeds, but he told them to wait until harvest to pull up anything because he didn't want to take a chance on uprooting a good plant by mistake. At harvest time, he said, I'll tell the reapers to collect the weeds and burn them but gather the wheat and put it in my barn."

This parable must have gone over the heads of a lot of people in the crowd, because later in the day, hours later, the disciples were *still* puzzling over it. Matthew tells us that after everyone else had gone home, the disciples pulled Jesus aside. "That parable about the weeds? We didn't get it, Jesus. Can you explain that one?" (Wouldn't that be great? To be able to ask Jesus for further clarification? "Um, say a little more about that, Jesus; you're not making sense.") So Jesus patiently deconstructs the parable: the farmer is the Son of Man; the field is the world; the good seed are the children of the kingdom; the weeds are the children of the evil one; the devil is the one who sows the weeds; the harvest is the end of the age; the reapers are the angels. "Just as the weeds are collected and burned up with fire, so will it be at the end of the age," says Jesus. "The Son of Man will send his angels, and they will collect out of his kingdom all causes of sin and all evildoers, and they will throw them into the furnace of fire, where there will be weeping and gnashing of teeth. Then the righteous will shine like the sun in the kingdom of the Father. Let anyone with ears listen!"

What we've got here seems to be a judgment parable. The kingdom of heaven is like this: some are wheat, some are weeds; the wheat goes to the barn, the weeds go into the fire. End of story.

The fact that it's typically pretty easy for most people—with the possible exception of lazy ten-year-olds—to distinguish between wheat and weeds is, I think, what makes this judgment call uncomfortable. My first reaction to hearing this parable is to say, "Well, of course, *I'm* wheat. Feel sorry for those poor weeds." My first reaction, though, is immediately second-guessed: "Maybe I'm not wheat. Maybe I'm really a weed. I know what a lousy person I really am, all the bad things I do. Maybe I'm not wheat; maybe I'm a weed— destined for the furnace of fire where there will be weeping and gnashing of teeth." What at first glance seems like an easy judgment call—weed or wheat—instead quickly becomes a troubling question. This ambiguity is unsettling. Where, really, do we fit into this parable about the kingdom of heaven? It's an uncomfortable question, especially in light of the judgment that so clearly punctuates the story.

The good news, though, is that this isn't *just* a parable about judgment. It's also a parable about patience and grace. Notice the difference between the way the servants react to the discovery of weeds in the fields and the response of the Master. The servants find the weeds and they're ready to pull them up. "There are weeds out there," they say. "Do you want us to go out and gather them up?" Industrious and hard working, these servants see something that doesn't belong, and they want to fix it and make it right. Keep those fields pure. There are weeds out there—do you want us to get rid of them?

Like these servants, we're pretty sure we know what weeds look like. We're pretty sure we know how to exercise judgment, how to separate the people of this world into categories, types, groups: good and evil, right and wrong, pure and corrupt, true and false, patriotic and unpatriotic, faithful and heathen, wheat and weeds. We have a feeling—call it intuition, call it a hunch—but we're pretty sure of who's who and what's what. Those who think, behave, vote, pray, and love like us, we treat *one* way; those who don't, we treat *another* way. We're quick to stick up for what we've judged to be wheat. We're quick to condemn—or, at the very least, to leave alone and unprotected and subject to bullying and harassment—what we consider to be weeds. *We* may not actually be the ones digging up the weeds, making life miserable for those who, for whatever reason, don't conform to "the way things ought to be," but we're reluctant to get in the way of *others* who claim that they're simply trying to make the field nicer, safer, more pure and pristine. Nobody likes a weed. Nobody *normal,* that is.

In contrast to these eager-beaver servants, though, who are sure they can spot a weed in the field and are certain they know what to do with it, the Master is a patient farmer. "Don't pull those weeds up just yet," he tells the workers. "You might pick some wheat by mistake. Let them both grow together until harvest time. *Then* collect the weeds to be burned and gather the wheat into my barn." The Master is a patient farmer and he's also smart. If he tends his fields, takes care of them, and lets them grow to maturity, then he can make sure that the wheat really is wheat, and the weeds really are weeds. This farmer isn't going to make any hasty or premature judgments. After all, it *could* be that some of what, to the casual observer, appears to be weeds may turn out in the end to be productive wheat. This farmer's not willing to uproot even one stalk of wheat by mistake, and evidently he doesn't believe his servants are capable of error-free gardening.

You may have heard before the story of John Newton. He was an English slave trader back in the eighteenth century. The slave trade was brutal and it was inhumane. And John Newton made a pretty good living out of it, buying and selling other people. By anyone's estimation, John Newton looked a lot like a weed. But then something happened. Jesus saved John Newton. Turned his life around. Newton quit the slave trade and eventually became a Christian minister. He also wrote a hymn about his experience, telling about his transformed life and praising God for not giving up on him. You all know it. It's called "Amazing Grace." That was his testimony. "My memory is nearly gone," Newton said late in his life, "but I remember two things, that I am a great sinner, and that Christ is a great Savior."

What looks to us like weeds just may turn out to be wheat. We never know. And, really, that's the point. Like any good farmer, the Son of Man doesn't want to lose any of his good crop by mistake. Let the fields grow, says the Master, and when it's time, we'll separate the wheat from the weeds. Even for such a patient farmer, though, there *will* come a day of judgment. Have no doubt about that. The time for harvesting *will* arrive, and when that time comes, the weeds and the wheat *will* be harvested—one destined for oblivion, the other to shine like the sun in the kingdom of the Father.

So, despite the farmer's patience and the suggestion that the Son of Man makes no premature judgments, this is still an unsettling parable that Jesus tells. Conflicted reactions to this parable are entirely appropriate. Like all of Jesus' disciples, we're mixtures of good and evil. Sometimes we're faithful, sometimes we're not. One minute we're God's loyal disciples, the next we're living like sworn enemies of the kingdom. We're conflicted. When we're alone and we're quiet and we work up the courage to look at our lives honestly, we're going to find that our hearts are like fields full of good, healthy wheat—with tons of ugly weeds popping up here and there all over the place. At our best, we recognize the conflict in ourselves and we recognize it in others. It's hard enough to understand what's going on inside of our *own* restless hearts, much less those of our neighbors, and acquaintances, and people we know about—and form opinions about—only from a distance. At our best, we know better than to try to play gardener, forcing others to conform to our ways, our opinions, our beliefs—or pay a price for refusing. The hard work of making judgments: at our best, we're willing to leave that up to the Lord.

Where does that leave us, then? Are we just supposed to spend our lives waiting with fear and trembling for the final harvest to come at the end of the age, unsure of whether we're destined to burn in the fire or shine like the sun? That doesn't sound to me like the abundant life that Jesus promises to his disciples. He came to set us free from fear. He came to set us free to *live*, not to be tortured, either with angst about ourselves or anger about others. Those with ears to hear can listen to this parable and be assured that the Son of Man is patient in making his judgments and allows weeds like John Newton, or me, or you, to grow in grace and, in time, be transformed by the power of his Holy Spirit. The Son makes his judgments so we don't have to.

Not only is the Son of Man patient but, as Frederick Buechner reminds us, the great good news of our faith is that Christians can look toward the harvest with confidence, knowing that the One who judges us most finally is also the One who loves us most fully—Jesus Christ, God's only Son, who lived, died, and rose again so that, in him, we might shine forever like the sun in the kingdom of the Father. Amen.

Living in Light of What We Have Read Together

These are strange days indeed for freedom-loving heirs of the early English Baptist tradition. As the world gets smaller, figuratively speaking, thanks to advances in technology, communication, and travel, it's becoming harder and harder to avoid people who think, behave, and worship differently than we do and have their own, legitimate, deeply held convictions as to why their way is the right way. To borrow and modify a metaphor from Jesus, it's almost impossible anymore for folks to spend their entire lives in one, single field that's populated exclusively by just one, single variety of plant. (As an aside, I'm not sure that such uniformity ever really *was* possible. Even in the smallest, geographically most remote, and seemingly most homogeneous villages in the Western world, I suspect that not far below the surface of apparent sameness, a great deal of moral, religious, and political diversity has always existed. That's simply how people are. Just because we don't remember seeing that diversity doesn't mean it wasn't there. Homosexuals were around, for example, long before the gay rights movement helped them become a more visible presence in our communities.) Add racial, national, and ethnic diversities to the aforementioned mix and, suddenly, it becomes a challenge for people to say precisely just who it is they're referring to when they say "we."

Obviously, this new reality (new, at least, in the sense that it's no longer possible to pretend that it doesn't exist) affects the way in which spiritual descendants of the seventeenth-century English Baptists think about, and practice, religious liberty. If the religious spectrum is, as American sociologist Will Herberg famously described it in 1955, largely a matter of "Protestant, Catholic, Jew," then it's not too much of a stretch for Baptists to be generous in their embrace of diversity, especially in a culture where they belong to the "in-crowd."[35] A few "weeds" here and there don't seem all that threatening when surrounded by acres and acres of robust "wheat." A religious spectrum that's wide enough to include Muslims, Mormons, Wiccans, Buddhists, Hindus, Jehovah's Witnesses, and those who adhere to all sorts of other belief systems, not to mention the rapidly increasing tribe of "nones"—that is, people who profess no religious identity at all—is a religious spectrum that's bound to generate some anxiety among Baptists who are used to dealing with such diversity only in the abstract. It's not hard to be tolerant of people who are different from you when they live halfway around the world. What happens, however, when the growing Muslim community in your town wants to build a mosque around the corner from your church?

Baptists in the United States of the twenty-first century, of course, will approach the question from a substantially different perspective than that of their seventeenth-century ancestors in England. The latter argued for religious liberty from a position of weakness. They simply wanted to practice their Christian faith in peace, without fear of persecution or coercion by the established civil and religious authorities. Their argument: You may think we're weeds, but Jesus says to let the weeds grow unmolested and leave the judgment up to God. For contemporary Baptists who most certainly don't think of themselves as weeds, and already feel as though the fields around them are getting uncomfortably crowded with unfamiliar plants, that position can sound pretty risky. Arguing for religious liberty from a position of relative (albeit declining) strength, and defending others from persecution on account of their religion—whether that persecution takes the form of slanderous gossip, discriminatory zoning laws, or outright physical violence—requires a great deal of grit, precisely because it's so unselfish.

In this newly competitive and disorienting, diverse religious marketplace, it's tempting to forget the convictions of our ancestors, scrambling to secure our own turf by making it more difficult for people of other faith traditions to worship and practice their beliefs as they see fit. We may be inclined to use whatever legal means are at our disposal to send the message—implicitly in some cases, explicitly in others—that, "non-Christians are not welcome here." That's one option. Or we may be tempted to forget the convictions of our ancestors by labeling any and all religious truth claims as arrogant and judgmental, insisting that there are no weeds to be bundled but rather many different, but equally valid, roads leading to the same Ultimate Being that some have traditionally called "God." While the message sent here accomplishes the impressive feat of patronizing both people of Trinitarian Christian faith and people of other faiths at the same time, it does represent another option for dealing with the reality of religious diversity.

The early English Baptists, however, show us another, more excellent way to live out the faith conviction that persecution on account of religion is wrong—one that is both generous toward others and faithful to the gospel we have received, and accepted, as truth. The best way to describe it might be with an old-fashioned word: hospitality. It is the traditional Christian practice of welcoming strangers and graciously making room for unexpected guests. On the one hand, Jesus' parable of the wheat and the weeds teaches us that, because only the Son of Man has the authority to make a judgment call on what he sees growing in the field, his servants are to allow every plant there to grow unmolested—they are, as author Robert Farrar Capon suggests, to practice a "letting be" that reflects a deep, abiding trust in God.[36] This means not only learning to live with religious diversity (that is, being tolerant of those whose beliefs about "ultimate concerns," as theologian Paul Tillich might put it, differ from ours) but also doing our part to ensure that people of all faiths (and of *no* faith) can worship freely and without fear of harassment.

In order to be hospitable toward your Muslim neighbors, then, members of your church might show up to the city council meeting to protest an unjust zoning ordinance prohibiting construction of that mosque around the corner from your own house of worship. Or you might simply invite your Muslim neighbors to a meal in your church's fellowship hall as a way of forming friendships, building community, and expressing support for their legitimate desire to worship together according to the dictates of their consciences. Extending hospitality to others in Jesus' name is not the same thing as agreeing with their ideas, endorsing their opinions, or giving credence to their beliefs. It is, rather, how Christians practice what Jesus preaches when he instructs his followers to let all the plants in the field grow together for the time being. In this sense, hospitality is the exact opposite of discrimination.

On the other hand, though, Jesus' parable also teaches us that weeds do exist and there will come a time when those weeds are, at the Son of Man's discretion, bundled and burned. What do we believe? How do we live? Whom do we trust? For the early English Baptists, these questions addressed matters of eternal significance—and there *were*, in fact, right and wrong answers. Faith wasn't a both/and proposition; it was either/or. This conviction, too, is part of the inheritance we've received from our seventeenth-century spiritual ancestors, and we mustn't neglect it out of fear of seeming judgmental or self-righteous. It is, rather, the driving force behind not only evangelism but also Christian education, discipleship training, preaching, caring for the poor and vulnerable—really, the church's entire *mission* in the world flows from the conviction that Jesus is the way, the truth, and the life, and God has chosen to redeem creation through him and the obedient work of his followers. If we didn't believe that the good news of Jesus mattered, then we wouldn't bother sharing it. But we *do* believe it matters and we *do* share it—not because we think we're "better" than those who aren't Christians but rather because we want them to experience for themselves the joy of abundant life and the assurance of eternal life that we've found in our relationship with Christ.

So how do our own faith convictions shape the way in which we practice Christian hospitality with people of other faiths (or of no faith)? In short, they challenge us to be honest about what we believe, and why—while at the same time being good neighbors to people who don't share our beliefs. They force us to think clearly, and deliberately, about how far we can accommodate others before we start compromising our own deeply held principles. What if the Muslim community in your town asks to use your church's fellowship hall for worship until their mosque gets built? Practicing generous, faithful hospitality can be a tough balancing act. Publicly express your own faith convictions, and you may get accused of being intolerant. Publicly stand up for the religious freedom of non-Christians, and you might get accused of caving in to the peer pressure of "political correctness." Few of us get it right all—or even most—of the time. The important thing, though, is to try.

As the apostle Paul writes in Romans 12:18, "if it is possible, so far as it depends on you, live peaceably with all." It is, indeed, by making the effort to be faithful Christians while also protecting space for non-Christians to live, work, play, worship, and flourish in our communities, that we best honor our seventeenth-century Baptist ancestors and their conviction that persecution on account of religion is wrong. They arrived at this article of faith through their reading of Scripture. When Jesus used the parable of the wheat and the weeds to instruct his disciples on how they should respond to the fact that not all people will believe Jesus' message about the kingdom of God and accept it as divine truth, the early English Baptists took these instructions seriously, applied them to their own circumstances, and then grounded their argument against coercion and persecution in what they heard Jesus saying. Four centuries later, their spiritual descendants will do well, when talking about the reality of religious diversity, to begin their conversations in the same place.

Notes

1. From the Declaration of Breda, as found in Earl of Clarendon, *The History of the Rebellion and Civil Wars in England*, ed. W. D. McCray, vol. 6 (Oxford: Clarendon Press, 1888) 206ff.

2. B. R. White, *The English Baptists of the 17th Century* (Didcot: The Baptist Historical Society, 1983; repr., 1996) 96.

3. John Sturgion, *A Plea for Toleration of Opinions and Persuasions in Matters of Religion* (London: S. Dover, for Francis Smith, 1661) 5.

4. Ibid, 12.

5. John Coffey, *Persecution and Toleration in Protestant England, 1558–1689* (Harlow, England: Longman, 2000) 67.

6. Sturgion, *Plea for Toleration of Opinions and Persuasions*, 15.

7. See Thomas Crosby, *The History of the English Baptists*, vol. 3 (London: John Robinson et al., 1740) 89.

8. Thomas Monck, Joseph Wright, George Hammons, William Jeffrey, Francis Stanley, William Reynolds, and Francis Smith, "Sion's Groans for Her Distressed," in Crosby, *History of English Baptists*, vol. 2 (London: John Robinson et al., 1739) 99. Underhill provides some helpful biographical information about these men. Monck, a pastor in Buckinghamshire, is generally regarded as the author of the General Baptists' Orthodox Creed (1678). Wright, "a zealous preacher of the gospel and a faithful sufferer in the cause of non-conformity," was known for his great piety and learning. Hammons and Jeffrey also helped write a similar petition to the king while imprisoned at Maidstone on account of their Baptist beliefs. Stanley served a church in Ravensthorpe, while Reynolds was sent by the church in Stamford to go "into the west for the work of the ministry." Finally, Smith was a printer and a preacher who made a huge contribution to the cause of

religious liberty by making Baptist writings available throughout England. Many of the tracts cited in this book were printed in his shop. For more detailed information on these men, please see E. B. Underhill, *Tracts of Liberty of Conscience and Persecution, 1614–1661* (London: J. Haddon, 1846) 345–47.

9. Monck et al., "Sion's Groans," in Crosby, *History of English Baptists*, 2:110.

10. Jeffrey, et al., "An Humble Petition and Representation" in Underhill, *Tracts of Liberty*, 303.

11. Busher, "Religion's Peace," in Underhill, *Tracts of Liberty*, 30.

12. Monck et al., "Sion's Groans," in Crosby, *History of English Baptists*, 2:120.

13. Jeffrey et al., "An Humble Petition and Representation," in Underhill, *Tracts of Liberty*, 303.

14. Busher, "Religion's Peace," in Underhill, *Tracts of Liberty*, 24.

15. For a good overview of these seventeenth-century arguments for religious toleration in the English-speaking world, see *From Jamestown to Jefferson: The Evolution of Religious Freedom in Virginia*, ed. Paul Rasor and Richard E. Bond (Charlottesville: University of Virginia Press, 2011).

16. Sturgion, *Plea for Toleration of Opinions and Persuasions*, 10.

17. Murton, "Persecution for Religion Judged and Condemned," in Underhill, *Tracts of Liberty*, 120. The last two references Murton makes are to Jesus' words on the cross in Luke 23:34 and the martyr Stephen's cry just before his death in Acts 7:60.

18. Busher, "Religion's Peace," in Underhill, *Tracts of Liberty*, 18.

19. Jeffrey et al., "An Humble Petition and Representation," in Underhill, *Tracts of Liberty*, 302.

20. Monck et al., "Sion's Groans," in Crosby, *History of English Baptists*, 2:110–11.

21. Jeffrey et al., "An Humble Petition and Representation," in Underhill, *Tracts of Liberty*, 302.

22. See, for example, chapter VI of the Second London Confession (1677), which asserts that, because of original sin, all humans are "children of wrath, the servants of Sin, the subjects of death and all other miseries, spiritual, temporal, and eternal, unless the Lord Jesus sets them free," in William Lumpkin, *Baptist Confessions of Faith* (Valley Forge PA: Judson Press, 1959) 259. Also see article X of the Orthodox Creed (1678) in Lumpkin, stating that all people who reject the grace of Jesus "shall be punished with everlasting destruction in hell fire, with the fallen angels, or devils, and shall be fixed in an irrecoverable state of damnation, irrevocable under the wrath of God, they being the proper objects of it; and shall remain under his inexpressible wrath and justice, in inconceivable Torment, Soul and Body, to all Eternity."

23. Monck et al., "Sion's Groans," in Crosby, *History of English Baptists*, 2:114, emphasis added.

24. Robert Farrar Capon's insights on this parable are particularly helpful. See his *Parables of the Kingdom: Jesus' Left-Handed Approach to a Wrong-Headed World* (Grand Rapids MI: Zondervan Books, 1988) 97–109.

25. Lumpkin, *Baptist Confessions*, 232–33.

26. Roger Williams, *The Bloudy Tenent of Persecution* (1644), ed. E. B. Underhill (London: The Hanserd Knollys Society, 1848) 10.

27. William Lamont, "Pamphleteering, the Protestant Consensus, and the English Revolution," in *Freedom and the English Revolution: Essays in History and Literature*, ed. R. C. Richardson and G. M. Ridden (Manchester, England: Manchester University Press, 1986) 82.

28. Williams, *Bloudy Tenent*, 89.

29. John Murton, "An Humble Supplication to the King's Majesty" (1620), in Underhill, *Tracts of Liberty*, 215. The story about Murton writing with milk is found in Michael R. Watts, *The Dissenters: From the Reformation to the French Revolution* (Oxford: Clarendon Press, 1978) 50.

30. Monck et al., "Sion's Groans," in Crosby, *History of English Baptists*, 2:118.

31. Ibid., 118–19, emphasis added.

32. Jeffrey et al., "An Humble Petition and Representation," in Underhill, *Tracts of Liberty*, 302–303.

33. Ibid., 303.

34. Williams, *Bloudy Tenent*, 155.

35. For a fuller account of how Baptists became cultural insiders in the American South, see Rufus Spain's classic study, *At Ease in Zion: A Social History of Southern Baptists, 1865–1900* (Nashville: Vanderbilt University Press, 1967). Barry Hankins tells the story of how this position of strength began to erode in his book, *Uneasy in Babylon: Southern Baptist Conservatives and American Culture* (Tuscaloosa: University of Alabama Press, 2002).

36. Robert Farrar Capon, *Parables of the Kingdom: Jesus' Left-Handed Approach to a Wrong-Headed World* (Grand Rapids MI: Zondervan Books, 1988) 106.

Chapter 5

Conviction

Loyalty to the King, Obedience to God

Sometime around the year 1651, the Baptists in Lincolnshire, located north of London and east of Nottingham, decided that they could no longer agree to disagree over the proper way to baptize new believers. They had been meeting together since 1644, enduring "great persecutions in their names and substance, by unjust slanders and confiscations" because they rejected the Church of England's practice of allowing adult sponsors (or godparents) to answer questions of faith and doctrine on behalf of infants presented for baptism. In other words, they refused to baptize babies—and a lot of folks in Lincolnshire didn't appreciate this departure from the churchly norm. While united in their commitment to believer's baptism, these beleaguered dissenters split on the question of how best to administer it. Some in the congregation argued that a generous sprinkling of water was sufficient. Others insisted that only full immersion could satisfy the mandate of Scripture. In typically Baptist fashion, then, members of the church finally settled the dispute by choosing sides and forming two new congregations.[1]

By 1656, the pro-immersion splinter had chosen Thomas Grantham to be its new pastor. Grantham was twenty-two years old and had never before served a church as pastor. In fact, he was himself a Baptist of relatively recent vintage, having just been baptized in 1652.[2] Even for a seasoned pastor, Grantham's new position would have been challenging, for Lincolnshire remained generally hostile territory for Baptists (though, in fairness to Lincolnshire, it was probably no more hostile than anywhere else in England at the time).

There were, reports one historian, "mobs" of anti-Baptist rabble-rousers who regularly interrupted Grantham's church meetings, dragging worshipers outside and stoning them. Indeed, though the Lincolnshire Baptists

> were respected by some, yet others used them very uncivilly, in particular, the [Church of England] clergy who, by warrants, brought Mr Grantham and several others before the magistrates. But having nothing to support their accusations against them but forged stories and lies, the wisdom of the magistrates soon perceived their innocency and the malice of their persecutors, and therefore set them all at liberty.³

It's worth noting here that this doesn't appear to be an account of one isolated incident but rather a description of what life was like on an ongoing basis for Grantham and his fellow Baptist dissenters in Lincolnshire during the tumultuous middle years of the seventeenth century.

From an *ecclesiastical* perspective, of course, the problem with these Baptists was that they refused to conform to established church practices. This refusal may have been a cause for concern among the aforementioned Church of England clergy, but it hardly explains the violent passions that Baptist non-conformity inspired in the mobs of Lincolnshire. The real issue, instead, was not so much religious as it was *political*—namely, the tendency in seventeenth-century England, especially after the Restoration of Charles II in 1660, to equate any sort of religious dissent with treason. Deviating from cultural norms in seventeenth-century England was dangerous—and not only in Lincolnshire. Such behavior sparked anxious suspicions that were, on occasion, well justified. Writing in 1661 from his home in Reading, Baptist pastor John Sturgion clearly recognized the problem that he and his fellow dissenters faced. The same liberty of conscience that, in theory, allowed dissenters to meet together privately for the peaceful worship of God was being used by rebels and insurrectionists as cover for their own clandestine gatherings to plot against the government. Sturgion understood that, for Baptists and other genuinely *religious* dissenters, the consequences of such furtive, treasonous activity were as predictable as they were lamentable. "The innocent suffer for the guilty," he wrote in a petition addressed to the king, "and many of Your Majesty's loyal and obedient subjects are questioned and publicly suspected to their great prejudice in their reputations."[4] Admittedly, Sturgion continued, the king's officials had good reason to be concerned about insurrectionists in their midst. He insisted, however, that Baptists were hardly sympathetic to the idea of treason: "I cannot imagine how Your Majesty can be unsatisfied as to the innocency of the Baptized people and others who have not only disclaimed the wicked rebellion of said persons . . . but won't even let the thought of wickedness enter their minds."[5]

These assurances did little to relieve the government's fears, and official harassment of the Baptists continued. Grantham's encounters with the king's officials in Lincolnshire are particularly well documented. One frequently told tale recounts how a detachment of soldiers was sent to Grantham's church in 1664 for the purpose of "disarming" the dissenters. After bursting rudely into the meeting, the soldiers failed to find any weapons among those gathered for worship, so they proceeded to search some of the Baptists' homes and confiscated private goods. They then took Grantham, along with several other church leaders, and, in the words of one historian, "made them run like lacqueys by their horses' sides" as they traveled from town to town searching for more potential troublemakers.[6] That night, they stopped at an inn, where Grantham and the other prisoners were tied up in a way that prevented them from resting. From what it sounds like, however, sleep would have been hard to come by even without the forced discomfort, as the king's soldiers sat up all night "damning and screaming, drinking and singing, making the place like a hell to those devout and pious souls."[7] The next morning, the prisoners were taken to a local constable, who tried to trick them into saying something incriminating. When that didn't work, the constable asked the prisoners if they would, under oath, promise to conform in the future to the faith and practice prescribed by the Church of England. Some of the prisoners, "for fear of suffering," agreed to take the oath. The others, including Grantham, "had strength and courage enough to stand the trial, and so three of them ... were by strict command sent to jail, where they lay for half a year."[8] At no point in this process were Grantham and his fellow dissenters formally charged with a crime. When they were finally brought to trial, the judge refused to rule on the case and the sheriff set the three prisoners of conscience free.

This story illustrates the challenge that religious dissenters faced in an age of political insecurity. Why did the soldiers break up the Baptists' meeting? Not for religious reasons. Instead, their intent was to disarm the dissenters—the assumption being, of course, that anyone meeting together in private under the guise of "liberty of conscience" must be up to no good and, therefore, a potentially armed-and-dangerous threat to the kingdom's peace. Once in custody, Grantham and his fellow Baptists found the king's officials predisposed to treat them with suspicion, and the laws of England offering them little protection. In the constable's eyes, these dissenters may not have been stashing weapons at their so-called "church meeting," but their behavior nevertheless did not conform to the behavior expected from a loyal subject of the king. If they couldn't support the Church of England, then could these dissenters be trusted to support the head of that church—that is, the king—and, by extension, England itself?

That question had bedeviled Baptists in England for as long there had *been* Baptists in England. John Murton addressed the issue directly in a petition to King James I. "If I do take any authority away from the king's majesty, let me be worthy of any desert," he wrote in 1615, only three years after Thomas Helwys had formally organized the first Baptist congregation in the kingdom. Murton's refusal to recognize the king's authority over the church, however, was not a political protest but a religious conviction, and he tried to make that distinction abundantly clear. "But if I defend the authority of Christ Jesus over men's souls, which appertaineth to no mortal man whatsoever," he continued, "then know you that whosoever would rob him of that honor which is not of this world, he will tread them underfoot. Earthly authority belongeth to earthly kings. But spiritual authority belongeth to that one spiritual king, who is King of kings."[9] As is the case with most nuanced arguments, this one sounded more persuasive to Murton's fellow Baptists than it did to the king, who had little patience with what sounded like so much hair-splitting. Baptists who could only proclaim *partial* allegiance to the king could hardly expect to be *fully* trusted by his government.

Therein, then, lay the practical challenge, not only for Murton but also for the Baptists in England, such as Grantham, who came after him during the politically turbulent 1600s: How can we reassure the government of our allegiance while, at the same time, adamantly rejecting its authority over our consciences? How can we, in other words, establish our credibility as loyal dissenters in this kingdom? Is such a thing even possible? The early English Baptists believed it could be done. The Baptist prisoners in the Maidstone jail, for example, put it this way in 1660, insisting that their refusal to swear allegiance to the newly restored Charles II should be interpreted not as a sign of political disloyalty but rather of faithful obedience to Jesus' command in Matthew 5:34 against taking oaths. In fact, they assured the king, "God is our witness, who is the searcher of all hearts, we deny not this oath because we would not yield due subjection and obedience to thee and thy authority. For this we say in the presence of him that shall judge the quick and the dead, we do, without any deceit, promise to live peaceably under thy government." Moreover, they added, "in case anything should be by thee commanded in spiritual matters, wherein we cannot obey, we shall not then take up any carnal temporal weapon against thee or thy authority, but patiently suffer such punishment as shall be inflicted upon us for our consciences."[10]

In restless, nervous Restoration England, however, such expressions of loyalty were worth only slightly more than the paper on which they were written. As always, actions spoke louder than words. So Grantham, for one, believed that the best way for Baptists to demonstrate their obedience to the king's civil authority was by . . . being obedient. And open. And as public as possible about what they believed and why. In an effort to stamp out potentially treasonous activity, various acts of Parliament had severely restricted the freedom of dissenters to meet for worship and prayer. These measures, however, served only to drive non-conformists into hiding. "It is the Lord himself who hath ordered his people to convene or congregate for the better discharge of the great duties of prayer, preaching, and celebration of his other holy ordinances," wrote Grantham, noting that Jesus never set a limit on how many Christians could gather at one time and in one place for such holy purposes: "We see not how we can, with safety to our souls, conform to the limits thereby prescribed" by the king and his government.[11]

If conscientious believers were going to continue meeting regardless of the consequences, Grantham reasoned, then it made a lot more sense to let them meet out in the open, especially if the government was so worried about what might be happening behind closed doors. "Being also rationally persuaded that the more public and free men are to serve the Lord, the less danger [there is] of sedition," he insisted that, "with innocent hearts and pure hands (as to any designing sedition) in the strength of Christ," those with nothing to hide would be very glad to stop hiding.[12] Conscientious believers could then worship God freely and openly, leaving only the true rebels and insurrectionists to scurry around in secret. Grantham noted that Baptists in England were indeed committed to both God and country, in that order. "We consider our nation to be a Christian nation," he wrote, "and are much more happy here than we would be anywhere else." Nevertheless, Grantham and his fellow Baptists remained steadfast in their rejection of the Church of England's understanding of the Christian faith. We agree with Tertullian, he wrote, that Christians are not born, but made,

> and, therefore, we do not think that our mere birth of Christian parents does qualify us or give us actual right to Christ's ordinances; but to this end we believe and know that every person ought to have the Gospel preached, or some way known to them, and that a work of grace (or new birth) at least by a solemn profession must precede our baptismal covenant. To this, the Scriptures give full consent.[13]

Indeed, it was in Scripture that Grantham found not only divine sanction but also, and more important, a divine imperative for the kind of loyal dissent he so passionately advocated. As historian B. R. White observes, during "the huge and violent fluctuations" that beset England throughout the middle of the seventeenth century, Baptists began "to move in favor of the government in power, whatever that government should be."[14] Their justification for such a fluid sense of political allegiance? The Bible—specifically, passages such as Romans 13:1-7 and 1 Peter 2:13-17 that explicitly called for submission to established civil authority. These biblical injunctions, White writes, were obviously of great significance "among a people committed to a thoroughgoing obedience to New Testament teaching which they took as legal for all time."[15] To that end, in 1674, Grantham published a lengthy sermon on 1 Peter 2:17, a verse in which the apostle urges his readers to "Honor all men. Love brotherly fellowship. Fear God. Honor the king." Focusing his attention on the verse's last two commands, Grantham argued that faithful Christians not only *could* love God and be true to their country at the same time, but that Scripture *required* that dual allegiance. Titled *The Loyal Baptist*, the sermon—and Grantham's use of Scripture as justification for his position—merits closer attention from those of us interested in learning how to talk about religious liberty in a more distinctively Christian fashion.

To be sure, Grantham recognized the inevitable tension between the apostle's call to fear God while also honoring the king. On the one hand, he wrote, "Christians must have an awful fear of God before their eyes that in matters of religion they may serve him only and not provoke him by sinful courses, nor by the fear of man"—a reference to the danger of conforming to man-made laws that violate the dictates of conscience. On the other hand, however, "Christians are bound by gospel-rules to be good subjects to princes, to honor their persons, and *conscientiously* to obey their authority."[16] The challenge for the loyal Baptist lay crystallized in the word "conscientiously." Grantham used it not as a synonym for "diligently" or "devotedly" but rather as a way of distinguishing precisely the *kind* of obedience that Scripture expected Christians to offer their earthly sovereigns—namely, an obedience both defined and limited by conscience. In other words, "gospel-rules" demanded that Christians obey the powers of this world, but only as far as they could without compromising their spiritual integrity.

For Grantham, the weight of the second imperative—"honor the king"—rested almost wholly on the first. Fear of God does not result from our sin. Rather, it flows from our recognition of God's goodness to us and God's sovereignty over us. "We are more subject to err than Adam was," wrote Grantham, "for all grant that he had free-will and sufficiency of ability to stand had he used it. But though some of us hold that we have a liberty of will, yet we must all confess our power to be very small, without intervening Grace, either to resist temptation or to do the acts of righteousness."[17] Our utter, helpless dependency on God inspires the feelings of awe, respect, and vulnerability that are bound up together by the word "fear," not so much because we fear what God might do with us as we fear what we might do without God. Therefore, Grantham insisted, we must "fear God—that is, stand in awe of His majesty, worship and serve Him and only Him. This is God's right. We must only pay it to Him."[18] In all matters of religion, he continued, good Christians will "stick close to that which is right in the sight of God, however it may be countermanded by man."[19] This dependency on God made bold obedience to divine commands possible despite earthly opposition. "No worldly power can ever make void what God commands, nor make that lawful which God forbids," wrote Grantham. "God's will must be obeyed what troubles soever attend us from the princes of this world for so doing."[20]

For Grantham, then, the command in 1 Peter 2:17 to "honor the king" had to be understood in light of what it meant to fear God. As a rule, Christians were indeed obligated by Scripture to obey their legitimate earthly rulers and serve them loyally. Consider the fact, Grantham observed, that the king originally referred to in 1 Peter 2:17 was undoubtedly the Roman emperor, a heathen ruler who was "a great idolator in his religion."[21] Nevertheless, the verse still instructed Christians to honor him. Interestingly enough, Grantham's understanding of honor ruled out any public criticism of the king. Old Testament prophets may have corrected kings and spoke out against them in public, he wrote, but they were commissioned by God. Ordinary Christians who disagree with the king should not voice their opposition in public because, as the apostle Paul said in

Acts 23:5, "thou shalt not speak evil of the Ruler to thy people."[22] In light of Grantham's career as a prolific writer and preacher who often found himself on the wrong side of the king's law, this may at first seem to be a rather odd position for him to take. In his many critiques of England's religious laws, however, he always focused his attention on the laws themselves, not the lawgiver. Grantham never attacked the king's personal character. His example is instructive for those of us living in a much more *ad hominem* era.

The biblical obligation to honor the emperor applied also to the laws "properly made" by legitimate human authority. Christians, wrote Grantham, must obey the law. The voice of Scripture spoke clearly on this point. Nevertheless, the command was not absolute. A believer's duty to honor the emperor (or Caesar's contemporary equivalent) extended only so far as the law remained consistent— or, at least, not in conflict—with God's law. "The error of an ill law must be refused by all faithful men," Grantham insisted, "especially in matters of religion."[23] Because refusing an "ill law" for fear of God necessarily involved disobeying the emperor's command, Grantham felt it necessary to explain how Christians could take such action and still remain in compliance with the last imperative of 1 Peter 2:17. Anticipating by some 400 years the concept of nonviolent resistance advocated by Mahatma Gandhi in India, and Martin Luther King, Jr., in the United States, he urged Christians to respond to unjust laws with what he called "passive obedience"—that is, disobeying the law itself but accepting the civil punishment incurred as a result of the disobedient act.

Grantham insisted that his idea of "passive obedience" was not simply a noble way of describing dignity *in extremis*, as is the case when, for example, a felon walks to the gallows meekly and without protest. In that situation, he wrote, "the felon hath ordinarily nothing to choose but must necessarily die, whereas the suffering Christian has life and liberty offered if he will but worship so, or so."[24] By refusing to obey the law and accept the consequences, the Christian "chooses to suffer, than to do that which he conceives (at least) to be sin in the sight of God, that he may be a faithful witness for God, and therein a blessing to his prince and to his nation."[25] The Lord has commanded us to abstain from every appearance of evil, wrote Grantham, quoting 1 Thessalonians 5:22. "Wherefore, if the power shall be so unhappy as to command otherwise, as it fell out in the case of Nebuchadnezzar," he continued, "there the penalty must be patiently endured. And then the powers are still obeyed."[26] Loyal dissenters, then, remain *passive* in the sense that they do not actively obey an unjust law. By accepting the civil penalty for their failure to do what the law demands, however, they demonstrate their *obedience* to the law's authority—and, hence, to the lawgiver. In other words, passive obedience in the face of an unjust law allows faithful Christians to fear God and honor the emperor at the same time, keeping their consciences clear and, perhaps most important, bearing a powerful, public witness to God's truth.

Grantham ended the sermon by returning to Peter's conflicting—and yet, in Grantham's rendering, compatible—imperatives to fear God and honor the emperor. On the one hand, he urged his readers to "follow peace with all men and holiness; to study to be quiet, especially in troublesome times; to fear the Lord and the king, and meddle not with them that are given to change"—a reference to the rebels and insurrectionists popularly believed to be lurking in every meeting of conscientious religious dissenters. "Many have undone themselves by itching after changes in worldly government. God only knows what is best for you and for the nation," he wrote. "They that are weary of this are soon weary of that."[27] Instead of engaging in fruitless agitation and encouraging others to do likewise, Grantham advised that Christians who take the words of Scripture seriously "will bless God for your prince and for the peace you have enjoyed under him, and pray for him and for all who are in authority, that under them (if the will of God be so) you may lead quiet and peaceable lives in all godliness and honesty." He then drove the point home: "They that will not pray for all that are in authority do not fear God, for they condemn His word. They do not love, and so cannot honor, the king."[28]

Having made one final appeal for his fellow Baptists to honor the king, Grantham next offered words of encouragement and strength to those who, for fear of God, "are at present under sufferings for the conscientious performance of what you believe to be your duty toward God in matters of religion." "Humble yourselves under the mighty hand of God," he wrote, "and suffer patiently what trials it shall please God to exercise you under, that 'at the trial of your faith, being much more precious than gold that perishes (though it be tried with fire) might be found unto your praise, and honor, and glory at the appearing of Jesus Christ.'"[29]

When Thomas Grantham read 1 Peter 2:17, the tension he found there mirrored his own experience as a loyal subject of the king who was, nevertheless, bound to obey God above any and all human authority. In a perfect world, these two commitments would never clash. In Grantham's world, however, they clashed regularly, with the king of England's church demanding from Grantham a measure of devotion that his conscience simply could not deliver. No doubt the temptation was strong to obey one imperative at the expense of the other—to fear God, for example, and make common cause with radicals bent on overthrowing the king in the name of political, or religious, freedom; or to take the opposite approach and honor the king by performing public rituals that betrayed God-given faith convictions. There were indeed Baptists in seventeenth-century England who made these choices. Grantham, though, was not among them. If 1 Peter 2:17 could place "fear God" right beside "honor the emperor," with the expectation that faithful readers would obey both commands, then Grantham was determined to figure out how to do both—and he did, threading the needle in a way that allowed conscientious Baptists to be true to God while, at the same time, respecting the king's temporal authority. Grantham deeply respected Scripture and, by grounding his idea of passive obedience in 1 Peter 2:17, he worked *within* the parameters that Scripture established in order to work *out* an understanding of what it might mean to be a loyal dissenter in politically perilous times.

Reading 1 Peter 2:17 Together

The verse—or, really, the *fragment* of the verse—that inspired Thomas Grantham's reflections on being a loyal Baptist is situated within a larger work written to early Christians who were themselves very familiar with the push-and-pull between human loyalties and divine obligations. Most likely written sometime in the late first or early second century—and most likely *not* by the apostle Peter but rather by someone writing in his name and, thus, associating its message with Peter's apostolic authority—the letter of 1 Peter is, in its opening verse, addressed to the "strangers who dwell here and there" throughout Asia Minor, a territory roughly equivalent to present-day Turkey. Other translations of the verse refer to Peter's intended audience as "exiles," "aliens," "foreigners," "sojourners," or "temporary residents." Regardless of the precise way we choose to translate the Greek word παρεπιδήμοις, the point remains the same: Peter is writing to Christians who are not at home in this world because their true citizenship lies somewhere else. We'll come back to this claim shortly. For now, it's enough to note that, at the very beginning of his letter, Peter is waving a giant, bright red flag, letting us know that the advice, instruction, and encouragement that follows is addressed specifically to followers of Jesus who don't fully belong where they live.

Along with this idea that Christians are living as strangers, or exiles, in this world, chapter 1 introduces another, related theme that will play out in the letter: Christians can expect to face difficulties and challenges in this world as a result of their faith. The good news, Peter writes in 1:4-5, is that believers have an immortal and undefiled inheritance awaiting them in heaven, which is cause for rejoicing. That's important, he continues in verse 6, because "now for a season (if need require) you are now in heaviness through manifold temptations, that the trial of your faith, being much more precious than gold that perishes (though it be tried with fire) might be found unto your praise, and honor and glory at the appearing of Jesus Christ." Within the first six verses of 1 Peter, then, we're told that the following message will be of particular relevance to Christians whose commitment to Jesus has, for whatever reason, put them at odds with the world and caused them to endure hardships that they might otherwise have avoided.

It's not hard to see why early English Baptists such as Grantham might naturally have been drawn to 1 Peter. Though separated from Peter's original readers by great distances of time, space, and culture, these early Baptists must have found the apostle's words strangely, almost providentially, applicable to their own circumstances. Throughout most of the seventeenth century, Baptists in England had a choice: they could either conform to the religious duties prescribed by law and avoid suffering, or they could remain true to what they believed God demanded of them and deal with the potentially painful consequences of non-conformity. First Peter clearly recognizes that this sort of conscience-driven conflict can and does exist, which allowed Grantham and his fellow Baptists to see themselves and their own struggles reflected in Scripture. Moreover, in addition to offering this sense of biblical validation, 1 Peter speaks in both practical and redemptive terms to Christians trying to figure out how to live faithfully in the midst of the tensions that their religious commitments have generated. No wonder, then, that Grantham paid close attention to what Peter had to say.

In chapter 2, the letter's focus turns specifically to the question of how Christians should relate to those holding positions of earthly authority. Peter begins this part of his message by returning to the theme he introduced in 1 Peter 1:1, the idea that followers of Jesus are, while living in the world, exiled from their true home. Ordinarily, a person's identity is defined by where he or she lives—as in the case of citizenship, for example—or by his or her family relations, ethnic heritage, or even primary language. For Christians, insists Peter, none of these traditional markers of identity are definitive. *Their* homeland, *their* citizenship, the place where they truly *belong* is neither in nor of this world. Instead, Peter tells his readers in 1 Peter 2:9-10, "you are a chosen generation, a royal priesthood, a holy nation, a peculiar people," gathered from all the many nations of this world and given this new identity by God in order that "you should show forth the virtues of Him that has called you out of the darkness and into His marvelous light. Which in time past were not a people, yet are now the people of God." However your identity used to be defined, wherever your loyalties used to lie, whoever your sovereign used to be—once you become a Christian, Peter declares, all that changes. Now, by the grace of Jesus Christ, you belong to God and are God's people, living in this world for the purpose of bearing witness to God's true nature. In other words, the way you live should accurately reflect who God is and what God is about.

So what does all this mean as far as how Christians ought to deal with the ruling powers and authorities of this world? First, Peter urges them to conduct themselves in exemplary fashion, so that no one will have any legitimate reason to speak ill either of them or of their faith. "Dearly beloved, I beseech you," he writes in 2:11-12, "as strangers and pilgrims, abstain from fleshly lusts, which fight against the soul, and have your conversation honest among the Gentiles, that they which speak evil of you as of evil doers may by your good works which they shall see, glorify God in the day of the visitation." Peter then explains that exemplary conduct also includes respect for both the laws of the land and those charged with enforcing it. "Submit yourselves unto all manner ordinance of man for the Lord's sake, whether it be unto the king, as unto the superior, or unto governors, as unto them who are sent of him, for the punishment of evil doers and the praise of them that do well," he writes in 1 Peter 2:13-14. Peter's rationale for this sort of submission should sound familiar: "For so is the will of God, that by well doing you may put to silence the ignorance of the foolish men, as free, and not having the liberty for a cloak of maliciousness, but as the servants of God" (1 Pet 2:15-16).[31] By obeying the law and respecting civil authority, believers can silence their critics who, presumably, include words like "scofflaw" and "agitator" in their list of anti-Christian slanders. At least, that's—again—what Peter hopes will happen. In this context, Peter's warning in 1 Peter 2:16 against using "liberty for a cloak of maliciousness" may be addressing the same sort of suspicions that dogged English Baptists in the seventeenth century—namely, that non-conformists will inevitably use their civil freedom for subversive, disloyal purposes. Peter's message: Don't do it. Instead, use your freedom to serve God.

As Peter walks these "strangers and pilgrims" through his understanding of how they must live as followers of Jesus in a pagan world, it's worth noting that he's not calling for good conduct, submission to civil authorities, and responsible use of freedom simply because they are worthy endeavors in and of themselves. Peter wants his readers to live in this particular way for the sake of their Christian witness in the world. They are to perform good works because doing so will cause others to glorify God. They are to submit to the laws of the land because doing so will silence ignorant critics of the church. They are to use their freedom responsibly because doing so will be of service to God. In every instance, then, Peter is urging his fellow Christians to adopt conventional, even conformist, standards of behavior in order to make it easier for them to extend the mission and ministry of Jesus in an inhospitable environment. Doing the will of God, however, remains the overarching goal.

Simply put, it appears as though Peter is offering strategic advice appropriate to the circumstances in which these Christians find themselves—circumstances familiar to Thomas Grantham and his fellow English Baptists in the seventeenth century and, if we're honest, are probably pretty familiar to Christians in the twenty-first-century Western world as well. The assumption here is that submitting to the "ordinance of man" is, in fact, acting "for the Lord's sake"—that is, Christian obedience to civil authority is a means to an end. It serves the worthy purpose of glorifying God and furthering God's kingdom. In the case of 1 Peter, it's important to keep straight this distinction between *what* and *why*. As long as the *what* serves the *why*, then followers of Jesus can act in good conscience. It's when this relationship gets confused—when the *what* seems to be working against the *why*—that problems emerge. With the broader context of 1 Peter in mind, then, let's now take a closer look at the particular verse that Grantham found so helpful, 1 Peter 2:17.

The verse contains four short imperative statements. We'll take them in order. "Honor all men," Peter instructs his readers. The Greek verb he uses here, τιμαω, is related to an adjective conveying the qualities of value, cost, and esteem. In the form of a verb, then, the word might be best understood as the action by which we place a high value on someone or something else, treating that person or thing as a prized treasure to be held in great regard. Treat all men (and, we can safely assume, women as well) with honor, writes Peter. Consider everybody everywhere worthy of respect and dignity. Fair enough. The next imperative, however, narrows the scope of Peter's instruction: "Love brotherly fellowship." The verb Peter uses here is derived from the noun αγαπε, which is the Greek word for the kind of sacrificial, generous love that Jesus expects his followers to offer each other. For the sake of comparison, consider the new commandment that Jesus gives his disciples in John 13:34. Jesus uses the same verb in that verse as Peter uses here in his instructions about how Christians are to relate to one another within the community of faith. "Love" suggests a considerably more intimate, personal relationship than does the word "honor"—the crucial difference, perhaps, between a warm hug and a firm handshake. With this second imperative, then, Peter both narrows his focus—he's talking now about fellow Christians rather than all people—and ratchets up the level of emotional commitment required.

Peter's third imperative, "Fear God," sustains this intensity. The Greek verb φοβεω carries with it a sense of reverence and awe that forever teeters on the brink of being debilitating. Think of the frightened shepherds standing beneath a choir of angels; the stunned disciples filled with fear, first after Jesus calms the wind and the sea in Mark 4, and again after he walks across the water to join them in their boat in Mark 6; the scared-to-death friends of Jesus huddled behind locked doors in Jerusalem on the first Easter in John 20; or the spirit of wonder that comes upon the early church as the apostles perform deeds of power in Jesus' name. In each of these instances, New Testament writers all use words derived from the same root, φοβεω, though clearly the emotions they're describing are not all the sort of quivering-in-their-boots, filled-with-dread-and-foreboding that we generally associate with the word "fear." It's something else. It's the feeling of being in the presence of a power greater than ourselves that we can neither fully understand nor even partially control. C. S. Lewis nicely captures this sense of the word in his book *The Lion, the Witch, and the Wardrobe* when Susan and Lucy first learn that Aslan, the great king of Narnia, is a lion. Speaking to her hosts, Mr. and Mrs. Beaver,

> "Ooh," said Susan, "I'd thought he was a man. Is he—quite safe? I shall feel rather nervous about meeting a lion." . . .
> "That you will, dearie, and no mistake," said Mrs. Beaver. . . . "[If] there's anyone who can appear before Aslan without their knees knocking, they're either braver than most or just plain silly."
> "Then he isn't safe?" said Lucy.
> "Safe?" said Mr. Beaver. "Don't you hear what Mrs. Beaver tells you? Who said anything about safe? 'Course he isn't *safe*. But he's *good*. He's the King, I tell you."[32]

This, then, is how Peter urges his readers to approach God: with the careful reverence due to a powerful Being who is undeniably good, yet beyond our control and not at all predictable in his actions. In order to make such an approach, however, we've got to *trust* God's goodness more than we're *intimidated* by God's transcendent, unpredictable power—and that requires us to be in relationship with God. In order to "fear God" as Peter instructs them to, Peter's readers must know God well enough to believe that God has their best interests at heart, even if they don't completely understand *what* God is asking them to do or *why* God's asking them to do it. As the tortured, faithful Job so eloquently, and mysteriously, spoke of his own relationship to God, "Lo, though He slay me, yet I will trust in Him" (Job 13:15). There is, then, certainly a degree of respectful distance implied in Peter's command to fear God, but it's balanced by the sort of intimacy that makes such a relationship possible in the first place.

The last of these four imperatives, though, takes a step back from this level of emotional intensity. In fact, the verb Peter uses to describe how Christians should relate to their earthly rulers is the same one he uses to describe how they should treat all people in general: "Honor the king." Just as "love" substantially upped the relational ante from "honor" in the verse's first two commands, now "honor" relaxes the intensity generated by "fear." Peter has, in effect, embedded his instructions on how Christians are to engage in their most important relationships—that is, with fellow believers and with God—snugly within a more universal call to respect everyone everywhere, as well as those who hold positions of earthly authority. In Romans 13:1-7, the apostle Paul urges obedient submission to the princes and powers of this world on the grounds that God has specifically ordained them to maintain civic order and punish evil. In 1 Peter, however, kingship is presented as simply a given fact of life in the real world. Peter doesn't assign kings any special, divinely sanctioned status, nor does he suggest that they be treated as operating under a mandate from heaven. Instead, he urges Christians to respect, honor, and highly value the king just as they respect, honor, and highly value every other ordinary person—because that's exactly what the king is: an ordinary person.

Finally, it's worth noting that immediately following these four imperatives—and a verse about servants obeying their masters, which grates upon our modern sensibilities—Peter has this to say to his fellow Christians struggling to be faithful to God in a hostile environment: "For this is thank worthy, if a man for conscience toward God endure grief, suffering wrongfully. For what praise is it, if when ye be buffeted for your faults, ye take it patiently? But and if when ye do well, ye suffer wrong and take it patiently, this is acceptable to God" (1 Pet 2:19-20). The implication here is that faithful Christians who honor all people, love their fellow believers, fear God, and honor the king may yet, nevertheless, end up experiencing pain, testing, and turmoil in this world as a result of their commitment to Jesus.

Peter may be offering strategic advice about how to follow Jesus in difficult circumstances, but he's under no illusions that his advice will necessarily lead to a trouble-free existence. Far from it—and, really, that's not the point. These four imperatives, remember, are directed toward the same goal: glorifying God and furthering his kingdom. Any honor that we give to the king that doesn't bring glory to God is honor that misses the mark. The *what*, in other words, must always serve the *why*. For seventeenth-century Baptists in England such as Thomas Grantham, the witness of Scripture here in 1 Peter provided a bracing measure of clarity in a world that must have, on a daily basis, offered confusing and conflicting messages about loyalty, what it meant, and who deserved it. Fortunately, these English Baptists weren't left to conjure their arguments about such vital matters out of thin air. Instead, they relied on the gift of Scripture to be both their starting point and their guide in articulating their faith convictions about what it meant to be a loyal dissenter in seventeenth-century England. Four hundred years later, their spiritual descendants will do well to follow their lead.

Hearing 1 Peter 2:13-17, 19-25 Together

The congregation at Murfreesboro Baptist Church in Murfreesboro, North Carolina, heard a version of the following sermon on Sunday, 11 May 2014.

Exiles on Main Street
1 Peter 2:19-25

For the last few weeks in Sunday school, we've been spending time in 1 Peter, which is a good place to be this time of year. The letter was written either by the apostle Peter himself or by someone writing in his name and under his authority. It was written, we're told in chapter 1, verse 1, to Christians who are in exile: separated from their true home, living—for now—in a foreign land, where the customs and values and traditions and priorities are very different from what's done back home. Peter's most likely using the word "exile" here in a symbolic way to reflect the situation of these Christians whose true home, whose true citizenship, as Paul puts it in Philippians, is in heaven, but who are living here and now in a fallen world among people who don't worship God, don't respect his ways, and don't seek to follow his will. Peter's writing to Christians who, through the grace of Jesus Christ, belong to God, who know they came from him and will one day return to him, but for now they are away from home, living here, in the words of Stanley Hauerwas and Will Willimon, as "resident aliens" and experiencing on a daily basis the awkward tension that comes with being in a place where you don't fit in—at least not like you used to.

That's who Peter's writing to: men and women who have come to faith in Jesus Christ and, as a result, have been given new life—which means they've given up their old lives, left their old ways behind: the way they once were, the way they used to think, the way they'd been in the habit of doing things, the way they had treated others before. They've left their old, rebellious, selfish, sinful lives behind and claimed the life of Jesus as their salvation.

But, as those of us who've tried to make that break know from our own experience, leaving the old behind is never as neat and clean in practice as it sounds in theory. It's not like flipping a light switch or changing the channel—especially when we're surrounded every day by the world we've supposedly left behind but keeps calling our names and inviting us to come on back and pick up where we left off. Being a resident alien, being a Christian in exile, is a bit like trying to quit smoking while holding down a job in the stockroom at RJ Reynolds, or to lose weight while operating the glaze waterfall machine on the assembly line at Krispy Kreme.

In Christ and his resurrection, we've been given this new life—with new priorities, and new values, and new loyalties, and a new understanding of what it means to love the Lord and be true to him in everything we do—but the old ways don't give up without a fight, and we're surrounded by reminders of how and who and what we used to be. Peter's writing to folks who switched sides and changed allegiances—they once were lost, but now they're found—but are still living in the same places with the same people and the same environment and influences and temptations as before. He's writing, in other words, to Christians who are familiar with the tension between what was and what is that arises as a result of their commitment to Jesus as Lord. They're familiar with it because they experience it every day.

These weeks after Easter, then, are a particularly good time to listen to what Peter has to tell us. Resurrection has a way of highlighting this tension between what was and what is, the old life and the new. Our reading today from 1 Peter, chapter 2, speaks directly to this tension and to the potential consequences for Christians who try and remain faithful to Jesus in the midst of it all. On the one hand, Peter makes it clear that, under normal circumstances, Christians ought to, as he puts it in verse 13, "accept the authority of every human institution, whether of the emperor as supreme, or of governors, as sent by him to punish those who do wrong and praise those who do right." Ordinarily, the followers of Jesus in this world must live as loyal, law-abiding citizens, staying out of trouble and giving no one any good reason to slander or discredit the church of Jesus Christ. How are Christians to conduct themselves? Peter sums it up in four short sentences. Verse 17: "Honor everyone. Love the family of believers. Fear God. Honor the emperor."

On the other hand, of course, it's not always possible to fear God and honor the emperor—or king, or president, or prime minister, or Congress, or whoever it is that exercises earthly authority in the places where we live. We can't always fear God and honor the emperor at the same time. In fact, in verse 19, Peter suggests as much. There will be conflict, there will be tension—and, as a result, there will also be suffering. "It is a credit to you," he writes, "if, being aware of God, you endure pain while suffering unjustly."

The key phrase here is "while being aware of God," which is a pretty watered-down translation of the word Peter actually uses here. It refers to "moral conscience," which traditionally, for Christians, has been equated with the obligations placed on us by God: what the Lord wants from his people, expects from his people, demands from his people. Christians traditionally have understood that our moral conscience is where, in a practical, everyday sense, the Lord pushes us in his direction. Now, I say traditionally because we've come to associate conscience with our own, individual little private voice telling us what we think is right for us, independent of any other consideration—an understanding of conscience that could not be further from the way Peter's using the word here. So a better way for us to read verse 19 is like this: it's a credit to you if, acting under the moral obligation placed upon you by God, you endure pain while suffering unjustly. In other words, Peter's telling us that if we're doing what's right in obedience to God, then we are to be commended for paying whatever price is demanded from us as a result.

What Peter takes for granted is the fact that folks who honestly try to practice what Jesus preaches are inevitably going to run into some sort of trouble, because the way of Jesus is at odds with the way of world. There will be times, Peter warns us, that the Lord will burden our conscience, will expect something from us, will place a moral obligation on us to do what's right in obedience to his command and for the sake of his kingdom and its priorities. It could be something public, like taking a stand on a particular issue or calling attention to an injustice. It could be something more private, like passing up a business opportunity because it takes advantage of the weak, or ending an unhealthy relationship that's causing you to compromise your convictions. But it's going to happen. You'll feel it in your heart, feel it in your gut: the Lord leaning on you to be true and faithful in your commitment to him, his way of doing justice, seeking righteousness, and making peace and acting in a generous spirit of love.

It's going to happen—it has happened. I daresay most of us in this room know the feeling I'm talking about . . . and we don't like it. It makes us squirm, makes us anxious, uneasy, because we're painfully aware that obeying God in this particular matter of conscience is going to require some sort of sacrifice from us. Whether it's profit we lose, the approval of our peers, our social status, a relationship we value, our own sense of comfort and stability—whatever it is we would rather have been doing instead—the opportunity cost us, what we give up in order to do the right thing. When the Lord stirs our conscience, we tend to get nervous—I know I do—because we have a pretty good idea of what obedience is going to cost us.

I knew a guy in divinity school whose aunt and uncle were Quakers and very committed, passionately committed to the Quaker doctrine of pacifism, meaning the refusal to participate at all in violence of any kind. As a result of their convictions about pacifism, they could not, in good conscience, pay taxes to support the Department of Defense and its military budget. So they voluntarily limited their income in order to live below the poverty line so they wouldn't be forced to pay taxes—and, as a matter of principle, they also refused to accept any government assistance like food stamps or Medicaid because they hadn't contributed to the system. I don't know how they did it, but they did it.

None of us are in a position to judge another person's conscience, but I do stand in awe of people like that who are willing to be obedient to God even when that obedience is costly—because I'm sure it wasn't just creature comforts and financial security they gave up. You know this aunt and uncle also had to deal with the sneers and scorn and contempt of folks who disagreed with what they were doing and were cruel about it. Verse 20: "If you endure when you do right and suffer for it," Peter writes, "then you have God's approval. For it is to this you have been called, because Christ also suffered for you, leaving you an example, so that you should follow in his steps." To follow Jesus is to obey God, and obeying God will put us at odds with the world. You can count on that. Like I said earlier, the world will put up a fight and do whatever it can to ensure that obedience seems like an awfully unpleasant option.

And, it's true: no one wants to suffer. Peter points to Jesus as the example for us to follow in this, but Jesus didn't want to suffer either. "Father," he prayed in the garden of Gethsemane not long before his arrest, "if you are willing, remove this cup from me. Yet not my will, but yours, be done." Jesus didn't want to suffer, but his desire to please God and serve God's divine purpose was stronger than his fear. Peter points to Jesus not as an example of someone who gladly suffered but rather as an example of someone who willingly obeyed, despite the risk, despite the cost, despite the consequences. This kind of obedience—not the suffering but the obedience—Peter assures us, pleases God and bears witness to his kingdom. What does God's will for his creation look like? The lives of obedient Christians: each one of them tells a story—a living, breathing, flesh-and-blood story of what happens, as Peter puts it in verse 24, when ordinary people are freed from sin to live for righteousness. They tell a story of what happens when those who were going astray like sheep return to the shepherd and guardian of their souls. The fact that these Christians choose to be obedient to God even when they suffer as a result of that choice—well, that makes their witness, their commitment, their love for God all the more compelling.

Jesus promises to equip us with what we need to be obedient when our time comes. By the power of his Holy Spirit, he promises to give us the words to say and the strength to love and the will to endure. He promises to be with us always, even to the end of the age. When God stirs our conscience, when we are called upon to do what's hard—but right—in obedience to the Lord's command, we will not be alone in that doing. Jesus will be faithful to us.

The unfortunate thing is, the sad thing is, we so rarely are willing to wait that long. We don't give Jesus a chance to be faithful. We don't give him the opportunity to keep his promises to us. Instead, we choose to bail out at the first sign of trouble. We'll cave at the first inconvenience, the first rumblings of discontent, the first evidence of a gathering storm heading our way. We don't hang in there long enough to give Jesus a chance to be faithful, to see us through—and our spirits are poorer, sadder, and weaker as a result.

"Danger and distress can only drive us closer to God," wrote German pastor and theologian Dietrich Bonhoeffer on August 21, 1944, from his cell in a Nazi prison camp. "It is certain that we can claim nothing for ourselves and yet may pray for everything. It is certain that our joy is hidden in our suffering, and our life in our death. It is certain that in all this we are in a fellowship that sustains us." Bonhoeffer had been given a faculty appointment at Union Theological Seminary in New York, but, burdened by conscience and in obedience to God, he chose to return to Germany in 1939 on the last scheduled steamer to cross the Atlantic in order to stand with his fellow confessing Christians in opposition to the Nazi regime. He knew what he was doing, knew the security he was leaving behind and the danger he was getting into, knew the price he might have to pay as a result of this decision.

For us, in our lives, the stakes may seem lower, but in the kingdom of God there really are no insignificant choices, no trivial decisions, when it comes to whether and how we will respond to the Lord's direction. Every day we are pushed and pulled, torn between what was and what is, the old life and the new. Every day, we make decisions about how we will live and who we will live for—and those decisions, they add up, they accumulate, and together they constitute our witness, our testimony, what we honestly believe to be true about God—not with our words but with our actions.

What Peter's telling us is, in a sense, what we already know: obeying God may get us into trouble with the world, and when that happens, we resident aliens, exiles on Main Street—in the world but, God willing, no longer *of* it—can take heart and be encouraged because Jesus has already gone there ahead of us. He's taken the worst punishment the world can dish out, and God has seen him through to the other side of the grave, victorious and alive forever. And God will see us through as well, God will be faithful to us in our obedience, just as he was to Jesus in his obedience. The resurrection is our assurance of that. "In Jesus," Bonhoeffer wrote in that same letter from August 1944, "God has said Yes and Amen to it all, and that Yes and Amen is the firm ground on which we stand." May it be so with us. Alleluia and Amen.

Living in Light of What We Have Read Together

A king is just a man. A queen is just a woman. Presidents, prime ministers, senators, representatives, governors, mayors, town council members: they're all just ordinary people who have been either appointed or elected to positions of civil authority. By virtue of their respective offices, however, they do have the power to make laws and enforce them, which means they also—indirectly, at least— have the power to inconvenience, fine, imprison, and even kill those who refuse to obey these laws. That's a lot of power, and power has a way of warping our sense of perspective and proportion, making ordinary people who hold positions of power seem much greater— *superhuman*, really—than they actually are. Extreme examples of this tendency, of course, are the cults of personality that form around dictators in autocratic regimes such as Nazi Germany and the Soviet Union in years past, or North Korea today. The same sort of thing happens, albeit on a much smaller and less dangerous scale, in other countries with other forms of government. It's natural to look up to our leaders. We want to believe that they are exceptionally wise, well informed, honest, and committed to the welfare of the people they are responsible for governing. We rightly have high expectations of our leaders, just as we rightly respect the positions they hold. Not surprisingly, then, it's easy to elevate these men and women to, well, *superhuman* status, believing that they are different, better, or somehow *more* than the rest of us. The truth is, though, that regardless of how successful or powerful he or she may be, every person who holds a position of earthly authority is still a flawed, fallen human being. Just like the rest of us.

It's good to remember this, lest we fall into the trap of confusing the laws that these flawed, fallen humans write with the will of God, as revealed both in Scripture and in the life of Jesus Christ. There *is* a difference. Just because something is legal doesn't mean it's right. American history is littered with examples of this distinction. The "peculiar institution" of slavery, the forced relocation of Native Americans in the nineteenth century, the Jim Crow regulations that segregated the South in the twentieth century, and the internment of Japanese-Americans on the West Coast during World War II—all these practices conformed to the laws of the land at the time, and yet few, if any, Americans today would argue (in public) that these practices were morally just. Surely, there are countless other, more obscure but no less painful examples to consider as well. While tragic and regrettable, the distinction between what's legal and what's right is deeply rooted in the fact that the laws of this world are necessarily drafted by sinners who—in a democracy, at least—have been elected by sinners. As theologian Reinhold Niebuhr frequently pointed out, this is the reality of life after Eden.[33] God is indeed redeeming creation and bringing it into line with his will, but a great deal of this holy work remains to be done. Until the Lord is finished with us, even the most well-intentioned leaders, acting with the highest degree of sincerity and good will, are going to get it wrong from time to time. That's the stubborn, unfortunate legacy of sin.

The point here is not to be unnecessarily bleak, much less cynical, about what we can or even should expect from the men and women who hold positions of civil authority. It is, rather, to underscore once again the fact that only *God* can be trusted, at all times and in every circumstance, to rule with perfect justice, mercy, righteousness, and truth. We don't have to worry about whether *God* is "getting it right." We can trust God to act always with integrity and in our best interests. Our only concern—and, admittedly, it's a big one—is whether *we* are acting in obedience to what, and how, and who God has called us to be, speaking to us, as God does, through the testimony of Scripture, the life of Jesus, and the demands of conscience.

We know what we're capable of apart from God's guidance, and so we ignore that guidance at our own peril. The problem, though, is that faithful obedience to God can generate peril of a different sort when God's expectations of us are at odds with what the laws of this world demand from us. Happily, for people governed by relatively enlightened individuals who create and enforce relatively enlightened laws, such conflict is rare—but it does happen. And *when* it happens, the early English Baptists teach us that Christians are free to say *no* to the king, the president, the state legislature, or whoever else is asking them to do what, in good conscience, they cannot do. There may well be a price to pay for saying no, but, in Christ, we do indeed have that freedom.

Now, for those of us accustomed to thinking about religious freedom primarily in terms of legal rights, the idea of paying a price—of any sort—for the sake of conscience may seem like a strange way to define freedom. Ordinarily, we understand that religious freedom provides protected space for believers to practice their faith without fear of government-sponsored coercion, interference, or penalty. There are, of course, limitations to this freedom—as is the case when one person's religiously motivated actions put someone else's health or safety at risk—but, generally speaking, we equate religious freedom with the right to live out our faith convictions as we so choose. If our religious beliefs bump up against the laws of the land, then we expect the laws to be flexible enough to accommodate us. We insist that we have a *right* to such accommodation.

What the early English Baptists knew from firsthand experience, though, is that the laws of the land don't always bend like we want them to. Sometimes they don't bend at all, thus putting people of faith in a difficult position, squeezed into what can be an agonizingly tight space between fearing God and honoring the king. The distinction between God's commands and those laws written by fallen, flawed human beings, however, gives Christians room to maneuver by giving them the freedom to disobey the latter in order to be true to the former. Our God doesn't just tolerate such disobedience. He encourages it. As a matter of fact, it's not too much of a stretch to say that God *expects* his faithful people to resist human laws that conflict with divine law. God expects us to do this—but God doesn't expect us to do it alone. He promises to stand with us, strengthen us, and sustain us through whatever trials and tribulations we must endure as a result of our resistance. (See the first six chapters in the book of Daniel for a biblical primer on what Thomas Grantham called "passive obedience" and divine deliverance.) God's ironclad guarantee that we are at liberty to obey him at all times and in all places is perhaps religious freedom in its purest form.

Now, it's true: the people reading this book will most likely never be threatened with a fine or a jail term, much less a beating or a death sentence, on account of their faith. We are fortunate. Unlike our early English Baptist ancestors, we experience very little friction between what the civil laws asks from us and God requires of us. If we're being honest, we should confess that this lack of friction probably reflects our willingness to go along in order to get along as much as it reflects the enlightened laws under which we live. On this side of heaven, we don't have to search very long or very hard for signs that the way things are in this world is not the way that God intended them to be. Usually, though, we're reluctant to say anything about these discrepancies for fear of seeming either odd, or obsessive, or just plain old ornery. Nevertheless, we *feel* the tension in a variety of ways. Indeed, because our consciences are not all shaped alike by the Holy Spirit, individual Christians are passionate about seeking God's justice and righteousness across a wide range of issues. Some people feel strongly about abortion, others feel strongly about peacemaking, others feel strongly about racial reconciliation, strengthening families, stewardship of creation, same-sex marriage, hunger, poverty—the list, truly, could go on and on. The point is, not every Christian is passionate about the same thing. Moreover, in keeping with the dictates of their consciences, Christians of good will and spiritual integrity, reading the same Bible and taking it seriously, can and do sometimes arrive at different, even conflicting, conclusions concerning the same issue. This apparent incoherence can seem confusing, especially for those looking for *the* Christian position on any given subject.

Baptists know better than to expect such uniform certainty in matters of conscience. We've spent our whole existence as a distinctive kind of Christian people insisting that every individual has the right to be wrong, even about matters of the utmost eternal importance. Don't be misled, however, into thinking that Baptists have *no* expectations when it comes to matters of conscience. We do. We believe that God expects us to read Scripture, pray often, worship regularly, pay attention to what our consciences are telling us—and then act accordingly. Maybe this means we end up on the wrong side of the law. If so, that's okay: God has given us the freedom to disobey unjust laws and will provide us with what we need in order to endure the consequences of our disobedience. For certain, though, this expectation that we act in fear of God and obedience to conscience demands that we tell the truth as the Lord has revealed it to us—and, in a fallen, flawed world that is still very much at odds with the kingdom of heaven, there's a word for people who are bound to fear God, honor all people, and tell the truth. We call them "dissenters."

What does this mean for *us*, several centuries after the early English Baptists first embraced the word "dissenter" as a sign of faithful, conscientious obedience to God? Perhaps it's time to draw some conclusions about loyal dissenters, reading Scripture, and talking about freedom in the seventeenth century—and what that legacy has to teach us four hundred years later.

Notes

1. Thomas Crosby, *The History of the English Baptists*, vol. 3 (London: John Robinson et al., 1740) 78ff. A later account describes the formation of what became Grantham's Lincolnshire church as not so much a split as a long process of attrition that, by 1651, had whittled the congregation down to four people committed to practicing immersion. See Joseph Ivimey, *A History of English Baptists*, vol. 2 (London: Button and Son et al., 1814) 263ff.

2. See Oscar C. Burdick, "Thomas Grantham," in *The Oxford Dictionary of National Biography*, ed. H. C. G. Matthew and Brian Harrison, vol. 23 (Oxford: Oxford University Press, 2004) 352.

3. Crosby, *History of the English Baptists*, 3:78.

4. John Sturgion, *A Plea for Toleration of Opinions and Persuasions in Matters of Religion* (London: S. Dover, for Francis Smith, 1661) 5.

5. Ibid.

6. Crosby, *History of the English Baptists*, 3:81.

7. Ibid.

8. Ibid.

9. Murton, "Persecution for Religion Judged and Condemned," in E. B. Underhill, *Tracts of Liberty of Conscience and Persecution, 1614–1661* (London: J. Haddon, 1846) 134.

10. Jeffrey, et al., "An Humble Petition and Representation" in Underhill, *Tracts of Liberty*, 307.

11. Thomas Grantham, *The Second Part of the Apology for the Baptized Believers* (London: n.p., 1684) 48.

12. Ibid., 51.

13. Ibid., 52.

14. B. R. White, *The English Baptists of the 17th Century* (Didcot: The Baptist Historical Society, 1983; repr., 1996) 55.

15. Ibid.

16. Thomas Grantham, *The Loyal Baptist, or An Apology for the Baptized Believers* (London: Thomas Fabian, 1674) 4, emphasis added.

17. Ibid., 21.

18. Ibid., 22.

19. Ibid.

20. Ibid., 25.

21. Ibid., 27.

22. Ibid., 32-33.

23. Ibid., 28.

24. Ibid., 36.

25. Ibid.

26. Ibid., 35.

27. Ibid., 39.

28. Ibid. Grantham here cites 1 Timothy 2:1-2: "I exhort therefore, that first of all supplications, prayers, intercessions, and giving of thanks be made for all men, for kings, and for all that are in authority, so that we may lead a quiet and peaceable life, in all godliness and holiness."

29. Ibid. Grantham is quoting here from 1 Peter 1:7.

30. For simplicity's sake, however, I'll refer here to the author of the letter as Peter. It makes for much easier reading.

31. The Geneva Bible translation of 1 Peter 2:16 is a bit hard to follow. Here is the New Revised Standard Version's translation of the verse: "As servants of God, live as free people, yet do not use your freedom as a pretext for evil."

32. C. S. Lewis, *The Lion, the Witch, and the Wardrobe* (New York: HarperCollins, 1994) 79–80, emphasis added.

33. It's difficult, Niebuhr wrote, to translate individual good intentions into widespread collective action because groups lack the capacity to subordinate their self-interest for the sake of others. This unfortunate reality, he concludes, is the residual effect of sin's corrupting influence on society. Niebuhr made this argument most famously in his *Moral Man and Immoral Society* (New York: Charles Scribner's Sons, 1932).

Conclusion

Getting It Right

Faith, Freedom, and a Distinctive Baptist Witness

> *Wherefore seeing we also are compassed about with so great a cloud of witnesses,*
> *let us lay aside every weight, and the sin which doth so easily beset,*
> *and let us run with patience the race that is set before us,*
> *Looking unto Jesus the author and finisher of faith;*
> *who for the joy that was set before him endured the cross, despising the shame,*
> *and is set down at the right hand of the throne of God. (Hebrews 12:1-2)*

This book began with the premise that, when English Baptists in the seventeenth century wanted to articulate their distinctive faith convictions—that is, to make their case for what they believed and why they believed it—they grounded their arguments in the words of Scripture. They didn't appeal to generalized biblical principles or universal notions of human rights. Such things did not yet exist, at least not in the way we now take for granted four centuries later. Instead, our early Baptist ancestors turned to the Bible for illumination, guidance, and instruction, and what they found there—specifically in the New Testament accounts of Jesus and the early church—became the basis for their efforts to persuade their fellow subjects that their understanding of Christian faith was, in fact, closer to the biblical model than any of the other alternatives.

It was an understanding rooted in the conviction that all people are free to respond to God's gracious offer of salvation through Jesus Christ. No one, they insisted, can become a true follower of Jesus without answering—freely, deliberately, and without coercion—Christ's invitation to "Come, follow me."

If this central conviction put the Baptists at odds with the established Church of England in the 1600s—and it did—then three other faith convictions, also derived from their reading of Scripture, served to sharpen the contrast even further. Given the turbulent, troubled mood of the country in those days, these three faith convictions—namely, that civil powers have no legitimate authority over matters of faith, that persecuting people for their religious beliefs is wrong, and that Christians must be obedient to the king in all civil affairs but only to God in matters of religion—arrived in England at the beginning of the seventeenth century packed tightly with theological and political dynamite. Challenging the king's authority over *any* area in which he claimed authority put a person in danger of being labeled either a rebel or a traitor. In such an anxious environment, where conformity and caution were public virtues, it took guts to be a non-conforming Baptist. It took even *more* guts to write pamphlets, publish sermons, and circulate petitions calling for the kind of religious freedom that Baptists believed best reflected God's will for humanity. The fact that these three Baptist faith convictions are now largely taken for granted in much of North America, Western Europe, and elsewhere is a testimony to the persuasive power—and persistence—of those who first championed them. The early English Baptists, it turns out, were *right*.

What matters for us, their spiritual descendants, is not just the fact that their understanding of religious liberty has been woven into the governing fabric of the United States and other like-minded liberal (in the classical sense of the word) countries. Of much greater importance is our ability to remember—and in some sense recover—the distinctively Christian witness that led our English Baptist ancestors to make their startling claims about faith and freedom in the first place. When they wanted to talk about freedom, they first read their Bibles—or, to put it perhaps more accurately, when the early Baptists read their Bibles, they ended up talking about freedom. This matters. It matters because, if we Baptists in the twenty-first century are going to continue lifting up religious freedom as one of our defining commitments as Christians, then we're going to have to get a lot better at explaining how this commitment is a particularly *Christian* commitment. That means more New Testament and less First Amendment, more Jesus and less Jefferson. That means, in other words, once again taking the Bible seriously as our starting point for talking about religious freedom without apologizing for it or feeling the need to package our distinctive faith convictions in the bland, secular language of universal human rights. The English Baptists of the seventeenth century have a great deal to teach us about how such vital work can be done, using Scripture not as a source for convenient proof-texts about freedom but rather as the starting point for deliberate, sustained, and humble engagement with God's written revelation to us. This book is a step in that direction, taken in hopes that others will follow.

Now, it's fair to ask, why is it so important that Baptists remember how to talk about religious freedom as a distinctively Christian faith conviction? As long as religious freedom is recognized as a universal human right—protected where it's been established and advocated where it's been denied—then why should anybody care how we describe it, much less how it reflects our shared understanding of God? The reason it's important for Baptists to be able to articulate their convictions about freedom and faith in deliberately theological language is because Baptists have, for years, insisted that a commitment to religious liberty is absolutely central to their identity as Christians and their witness to the world. There is indeed a powerful witness to God's sovereignty, God's love, God's mercy, God's patience, and God's faithfulness contained in the idea of religious freedom. It tells a compelling story about a Creator who loves us enough to let us make up our own minds about how we will respond to his offer of abundant life now and eternal life forever through Jesus Christ. It reminds us that the kingdom of God that Jesus proclaimed makes moral, spiritual, economic, and even political demands on us that are at odds with what the powers of this world expect from us—which means that our faithful obedience to God's kingdom way in the face of earthly opposition and hostility is a sign of his victory over these same powers. Finally, it reassures us that we are not alone in this world because the same God who speaks to us through his written word and the stirring of our conscience promises to both strengthen and sustain us when we must suffer on account of our faith.

Our historic commitment to religious freedom is not an accident. What we believe about faith and freedom is bound up in our understanding of the good news that God has freely chosen to redeem the world through the love of his Son, Jesus, and the creation of a faithful people called to live in obedience to his will. This is the Christian story. We call it the gospel of Jesus Christ, and, according to the particular way in which Baptists have told this story through the years, the God-given freedom that every person has to accept or reject this good news is an essential part of the story. If we can't talk about religious freedom in these terms, then we're failing to bear what we Baptists ourselves insist is our own distinctive Christian witness to the world. If our goal is simply to promote freedom of religion around the world, then allowing the First Amendment and other similarly inspired secular documents to do our heavy lifting makes sense. We can add our voices to the chorus of those who insist that human beings are, by their very nature, free to make up their own minds about what and how they will believe about God. We can then modestly stand aside, smile, and nod knowingly, reminding folks every now and then that, "This is, you know, primarily a *Baptist* achievement." I believe, however, that we can—and should—do better. We owe it to our early Baptist ancestors who struggled and suffered for their conviction that freedom does indeed have something to do with God's way of bringing salvation into this flawed, fallen world, that it's more about *God* than it is about *us*. We owe it also to those who haven't yet come to faith in Jesus. We have good news to share with them—and our convictions about religious freedom, we believe, are an essential part of that message.

That's why the title of this book is *The Loyal Dissenters*. We touched on the idea of what it means to be a dissenter at the end of the last chapter. Dissenters fear God, honor all people, and tell the truth as best they can—especially when the truth is contrary to the official government position, the majority view, or conventional wisdom. Dissenters listen to their consciences and do what they believe God is asking them to do. Often, they pay a price for their obedience. This was certainly the experience of Baptists in seventeenth-century England. They dissented from the king's laws concerning religion, rejecting his authority over matters of faith and charging that religious persecution violated God's will. Nevertheless, they remained steadfastly loyal subjects of the king. In fact, they went to great lengths to assure the king of their loyalty. For example, writes B. R. White, the General Baptists issued "A Brief Confession or Declaration of Faith" in 1660 "in order partly to shear themselves of suspicion that they were planning a violent uprising in London, and partly to show that their beliefs belonged to the Christian mainstream."[1] The confession's closing lines directly addressed rumors that Baptists were stockpiling weapons. The authors of the confession not only denied these reports but also proclaimed "that we do utterly abhor, and abominate the thoughts [of violent attacks] and much more the actions."[2] While some did participate in insurrectionist movements and clandestine plots, for the most part Baptists were not revolutionaries or rebels, nor were they traitors. Baptists may have been dissenters, but they were, overwhelmingly, *loyal* dissenters.

This is a crucial distinction that often gets lost in the angry backlash of reaction that dissent—of any kind, anytime, anywhere—tends to provoke. It was true in seventeenth-century England, when government officials and the general public alike assumed that non-conformity in religion went hand in hand with treasonous activity against the state. It remains true today in the United States, when dissenters are routinely labeled as unpatriotic, un-American, or worse. The same is true, no doubt, in other countries as well. A second premise of this book has been that, in addition to the ability to talk about religious freedom in distinctively Christian fashion, we can learn from the English Baptists of the seventeenth century about how to exercise our freedom in ways that are both truthful to God and redemptive for our fellow citizens. These early Baptists, in other words, can teach us something about what it means to be a loyal dissenter in the troubled, tumultuous twenty-first century.

In keeping with the example set for us by our spiritual ancestors, then, let's begin with Scripture and take a quick look at the Old Testament book of Jeremiah 29. The kingdom of Judah has been conquered by Nebuchadnezzar and his Babylonian armies. Jerusalem has been reduced to rubble. The best and the brightest of God's people have been carted off to Babylon, where their talents can be used to further the interests of Nebuchadnezzar's growing empire. Jeremiah, however, was not taken to Babylon. In fact, before the Babylonians crushed Jerusalem, the prophet had been thrown in jail by his fellow Israelites for predicting that the disobedience of God's people would soon lead to disaster. Released from prison by the Babylonians, Jeremiah settles not far from the ruined city of Jerusalem, in Mizpah. There, he begins to learn about the fate of God's people in exile—their sorrow, their suffering, and their uncertainty over what to do and how to proceed in this foreign land where they are now living. Should they rebel against the Babylonians? Should they cooperate with them? What is the faithful way for God's people to conduct themselves while living as strangers and aliens in exile? In response to their situation, Jeremiah writes them a letter, containing these instructions from God:

> Thus hath the LORD of hosts, the God of Israel spoken unto all that are carried away captives. . . . Build you houses to dwell in, and plant your gardens, and eat the fruits of them. Take you wives, and beget sons and daughters, and take wives for your sons and give your daughters to husbands, that they may bear sons and daughters, that you may be increased there and not diminished. *And seek the prosperity of the city where I have caused you to be carried away captives, and pray unto the LORD for it, for in the peace thereof shall you have peace.* (Jeremiah 29:4-7, emphasis added)

These words from the Lord to his people living as strangers in a strange land make it clear that God intends for his exiled people to invest themselves in the welfare of Babylon, to work for its success, and to contribute whatever they can to its peace and stability. In modern parlance, they are to act less like foreigners with tourist visas and more like good citizens, prepared to stay for a while in this strange land and make the best of it.

Now, remember the way in which the apostle Peter addressed his readers: he called them "strangers and pilgrims" (1 Pet 2:11). Other translations of this verse use the word "exiles" instead of "pilgrims." Most likely, Peter chose these words deliberately. By describing the early church in a way that hearkens back to the Israelites' experience of exile in Babylon, the apostle gives these Christians a different way of understanding themselves and their situation in the world—no longer a struggling, beleaguered minority but rather a brave community of God-fearing exiles keeping their faith in a hostile environment. With this in mind, Peter's instructions to the early church beginning with 1 Peter 2:12 start to sound a lot like the ones found in Jeremiah's letter to the Babylonian exiles. Do good. Obey the law. Avoid evil and those who engage in foolish behavior. In other words—again, as we might say—be good citizens. We probably shouldn't be surprised that English Baptists such as Thomas Grantham gravitated toward these verses from 1 Peter. It's sound advice for people whose *true* home may be elsewhere but who for now find themselves living among spiritual strangers.

As long as God's people are living in this world, they are away from the home that's been prepared for them in heaven. The Bible assures us, though, that the Lord doesn't abandon his people in exile. Instead, through the prophet Jeremiah, God gives us pretty clear directions: *Seek the prosperity of the city where I have caused you to be carried away as captives, and pray unto the* LORD *for it, for in the peace thereof shall you have peace.* Be good citizens. Serve the community and nation where you live, doing what you can to strengthen the common good and promote peace and prosperity. Peter understood this advice, and it shaped his instructions to the early church. The early Baptists in England seem to have understood it as well, and it shaped their loyalty to king and country. Even when persecuted on account of their religious non-conformity, they didn't waver in expressing publicly their respect for the crown and their devotion to England and its welfare.

They also seemed to understand, however, that seeking the welfare of a city—or state, or kingdom, or country—sometimes means that people of faith must speak out in dissent and be prepared to pay a price for it. When laws conflict with God's commands, when policies contradict the life and teachings of Jesus, when practices violate the dictates of a Spirit-led conscience, then faithful Christians are called to resist these laws, policies, and practices. The Lord expects us to dissent and, in doing so, bear witness to the truth we've been given to share. This is, once again, religious freedom in its purest form: the liberty we have in Christ to stand firm in our obedience to God. The early Baptists in England dissented because they could not, in good conscience, give to the king what rightly belonged to God alone—that is, their religious devotion. They also could not, in good conscience, allow such a grievous error to go unchallenged. If their fellow subjects, not to mention the king and his officials, were ever going to get it right, then first they needed to know that they were getting it wrong. So the Baptists dissented because their consciences demanded it, but they did so with the hope that, in time, the king and his officials would realize the error of their ways and change. Their dissent, in other words, was redemptive.

Do the spiritual descendants of these seventeenth-century Baptists have it in us to follow their example of loyal dissent? I'd like to think so. N. T. Wright, a New Testament scholar and Anglican bishop, once described the church's proper relationship to the state in a way that sounds very much like loyal dissent. "The task of the government in the present is to anticipate the eventual sorting out of things, and the task of the church in the present is to remind governments that that is their job," he said. "The resurrection gives you a sense of what God wants to do for the whole world, and it gives the church the courage to say, 'God's new world has actually begun already.'" The practical implications of this good news, Wright went on to say, determine the nature and the occasion for Christian witness in the public square: "The church can then say to the powers that be . . . 'We are urging you to do justice, and we're going to hold your feet to the fire and go on reminding you when you're getting it wrong and congratulating you when you're getting it right.'"[3]

I'd like to think that Baptists of good will are capable of offering this sort of public witness in the places where it's most needed, guided by conscience and informed by both Scripture and the life of Jesus. The Spirit will move us in different ways for different reasons. What's important is that when the Spirit *does* move us, we are willing to respond with obedience—and defend the freedom of others to respond as *they* are led. I'd also like to think that we can bear witness in a way that honors the spirit of Jeremiah 29:4-7, wisely balancing our obligation to seek the welfare of our cities with the realization that in this fallen, flawed world, there will always be ample cause for repentance, even when our leaders act with the best of intentions. Finally, I am confident that, if we ask, then God will gladly give us the graceful, generous spirits—not to mention the courage—we need to be loyal dissenters in the places where he has brought us to live as strangers and exiles for the time being.

Some four hundred years ago, a handful of free and faithful Christians in England showed us that it *can* be done. With God's help, perhaps the same may be said of us someday.

Notes

1. B. R. White, *The English Baptists of the 17th Century* (Didcot: The Baptist Historical Society, 1983; repr., 1996) 97.

2. "A Brief Confession or Declaration of Faith" (1660), which eventually came to be regarded as the Standard Confession for England's General Baptists, in William Lumpkin, *Baptist Confessions of Faith* (Valley Forge PA: Judson Press, 1959) 234.

3. N. T. Wright, interview with Lisa Miller and Jon Meacham, "Everything Old Is New Again," *Newsweek*, 5 May 2008, 20.

Bibliography

Barr, Beth Allison, Bill J. Leonard, Mikeal C. Parsons, and C. Douglas Weaver. *The Acts of the Apostles: Four Centuries of Baptist Interpretation.* Waco TX: Baylor University Press, 2009.

Bass, Clint C. "Thomas Grantham and General Baptist Theology." D.Phil. dissertation, University of Oxford, 2008.

Brackney, William. *Historical Dictionary of the Baptists.* Lanham MD: The Scarecrow Press, Ltd., 1999.

Bryson, Bill. *Shakespeare: The World as a Stage.* London: Harper Perennial, 2007.

Burdick, Oscar C. "Thomas Grantham." In *The Oxford Dictionary of National Biography*, edited by H. C. G. Matthew and Brian Harrison. Volume 23, page 352. Oxford: Oxford University Press, 2004.

Burrage, Champlain. *The Early English Dissenters.* Volume 1. Cambridge: Cambridge University Press, 1912.

Calvin, John. *Institutes of the Christian Religion.* Edited by John T. McNeil. Translated by Ford Lewis Battles. Philadelphia: Westminster Press, 1960.

Capon, Robert Farrar. *Parables of the Kingdom: Jesus' Left-Handed Approach to a Wrong-Headed World.* Grand Rapids MI: Zondervan Books, 1988.

Carter, Warren. *Seven Events that Shaped the New Testament World.* Grand Rapids MI: Baker Books, 2013.

Chadwick, Henry. "Augustine." In *Founders of Thought: Plato, Aristotle, Augustine.* Oxford: Oxford University Press, 1991. 191–297.

Clarendon, Edward Hyde, 1st Earl of (1609–74). *The History of the Rebellion and Civil Wars in England,* edited by W. D. McCray, 6 volumes. Oxford: Clarendon Press, 1888.

Coffey, John. *Persecution and Toleration in Protestant England, 1558–1689.* Harlow: Longman, 2000.

Crosby, Thomas. *The History of the English Baptists.* 4 volumes. London: John Robinson et al., 1738–1740.

Danvers, Henry. *Certain Quaeries Concerning Liberty of Conscience.* London: Giles Calvert, 1649.

Davis, J. C. "Religion and the Struggle for Freedom in the English Revolution." *The Historical Journal* 35 (1992): 507–30.

Dunn, James. "The Baptist Vision of Religious Liberty." In *Proclaiming the Baptist Vision: Religious Liberty,* edited by Walter B. Shurden, 31–37. Macon GA: Smyth and Helwys, 1997.

First Freedom: The Baptist Perspective on Religious Liberty, edited by Thomas White, Jason G. Duesing, and Malcolm B. Yarnell. Nashville: B&H Publishing Group, 2007.

Fletcher, Anthony. "The Enforcement of the Conventicle Acts, 1664-1679." In *Persecution and Toleration,* edited by W. J. Sheils, 235–46. Oxford: Basil Blackwell, 1984.

Gonzales, Justo L. *The Story of Christianity: Vol. 2, The Reformation to the Present Day.* San Francisco: HarperCollins, 1985.

Grant, Robert M. *A Short History of the Interpretation of the Bible*. 2nd ed. London: SCM Press, 1984.

Grantham, Thomas. *Christianismus Primitivus*. London: Francis Smith, 1678.

———. *The Loyal Baptist, or An Apology for the Baptized Believers*. London: Thomas Fabian, 1674.

———. *The Prisoner Against the Prelate, or A Dialogue Between the Common Gaol and Cathedral of Lincoln*. N.p.: n.p.p., 1662.

———. *The Second Part of the Apology for the Baptized Believers*. London: no publisher, 1684.

Greaves, Richard L. "Henry Danvers." In *The Oxford Dictionary of National Biography*, edited by H. C. G. Matthew and Brian Harrison, volume 15, 100. Oxford: Oxford University Press, 2004.

Grenz, Stanley. *A Primer on Postmodernism*. Grand Rapids MI: Eerdmans Publishing Company, 1996.

Hankins, Barry. *Uneasy in Babylon: Southern Baptist Conservatives and American Culture*. Tuscaloosa: University of Alabama Press, 2002.

Hill, Christopher. *The World Turned Upside Down: Radical Ideas During the English Revolution*. London: Penguin Books, 1972.

Hughey, J. D. "The Theological Frame of Religious Liberty." *Christian Century*, 6 November 1963.

Ivimey, Joseph. *A History of English Baptists, Volume 1*. London: Burditt, Button et al., 1811.

Johnson, Luke Timothy. "Religious Rights and Christian Texts." In *Religious Human Rights in Global Perspectives*, edited by John Witte, Jr., and Johan van der Vyver, 65–96. Boston: M. Nijhoff, 1996.

Keach, Benjamin. *The Baptist Catechism, or A Brief Instruction in the Principles of Christian Religion*, 16th ed. London: John Robinson, 1764.

Lamont, William. "Pamphleteering, the Protestant Consensus, and the English Revolution." In *Freedom and the English Revolution: Essays in History and Literature*, edited by R. C. Richardson and G. M. Ridden, 72–92. Manchester England: Manchester University Press, 1986.

LaTourette, Kenneth Scott. *A History of Christianity: Volume 1, Beginnings to 1500*. San Francisco: HarperCollins, 1975.

Lewis, C. S. *The Lion, the Witch, and the Wardrobe*. New York: HarperCollins, 1994.

Long, Thomas. *Matthew*. Louisville KY: Westminster John Knox Press, 1997.

Lumpkin, William. *Baptist Confessions of Faith*. Valley Forge PA: Judson Press, 1959.

Lundin, Roger. *The Culture of Interpretation: Christian Faith and the Post-Modern World*. Grand Rapids MI: Eerdmans Publishing Company, 1993.

MacIntyre, Alasdair. *Whose Justice? Which Rationality?* Notre Dame IN: University of Notre Dame Press, 1988.

McBeth, H. Leon. *The Baptist Heritage*. Nashville: Broadman Press, 1987.

———. *English Baptist Literature on Religious Liberty to 1689*. New York: Arno Press, 1980.

McClendon, James W., Jr. *Doctrine: Systematic Theology, Volume 2*. Nashville: Abingdon Press, 1994.

Miller, Lisa. "Everything Old Is New Again." *Newsweek*, 5 May 2008.

Monck, Thomas, Joseph Wright, George Hammons, William Jeffrey, Francis Stanley, William Reynolds, and Francis Smith. "Sion's Groans for Her Distressed." In Thomas Crosby, *The History of English Baptists*, volume 2, 99–130. London: John Robinson et al., 1739.

Niebuhr, Reinhold. *Moral Man and Immoral Society*. New York: Charles Scribner's Sons, 1932.

Nye, Joseph S., Jr., *Soft Power: The Means to Success in World Politics*. Jackson TN: Public Affairs, 2005.

O'Donovan, Oliver. *The Desire of the Nations: Rediscovering the Roots of Political Theology*. Cambridge: Cambridge University Press, 1996.

Rasor, Paul, and Richard E. Bond, editors. *From Jamestown to Jefferson: The Evolution of Religious Freedom in Virginia*. Charlottesville: University of Virginia Press, 2011.

Robinson, Henry. *John the Baptist, Forerunner of Jesus Christ, or A Necessity for Liberty of Conscience*. London: no publisher, 1644.

Shaw, W. A. Revised by Sean Kelsey. "Samuel Richardson." In *The Oxford Dictionary of National Biography*, edited by H. C. G. Matthew and Brian Harrison, volume 46, 845. Oxford: Oxford University Press, 2004.

Shurden, Walter B. *The Baptist Identity: Four Fragile Freedoms*. Macon GA: Smyth & Helwys, 1993.

———. "How We Got That Way." In *Proclaiming the Baptist Vision: Religious Liberty*, edited by Walter B. Shurden, 13–29. Macon GA: Smyth & Helwys, 1997.

Singman, Jeffery L. *Daily Life in Elizabethan England*. Westport CT: Greenwood Press, 1995.

Spain, Rufus. *At Ease in Zion: A Social History of Southern Baptists, 1865–1900*. Nashville: Vanderbilt University Press, 1967.

Sturgion, John. *A Plea for Toleration of Opinions and Persuasions in Matters of Religion.* London: S. Dover, for Francis Smith, 1661.

Taylor, Adam. *The History of the English General Baptists*, 2 volumes. London: T. Bore, 1818.

Thomas Aquinas. *Political Writings.* Edited by R. W. Dyson. Cambridge: Cambridge University Press, 2002.

Torbet, Robert G. *A History of the Baptists.* Philadelphia: Judson Press, 1950.

Underwood, A. C. *A History of the English Baptists.* London: Kingsgate Press, 1947.

Watts, Michael R. *The Dissenters: From the Reformation to the French Revolution.* Oxford: Clarendon Press, 1978.

Westphal, Merold. *Whose Community? Which Interpretation?: Philosophical Hermeneutics for the Church.* Grand Rapids MI: Baker Books, 2009.

White, B. R. *The English Baptists of the 17th Century.* Didcot: The Baptist Historical Society, 1983; reprint, 1996.

Williams, Roger. *The Bloudy Tenent of Persecution* (1644). Edited by E. B. Underhill. London: The Hanserd Knollys Society, 1848.

Wood, J. W. *A Condensed History of the General Baptists of the New Connexion.* London: Simpkin, Marshall, and Co., 1847.

Other available titles from  SMYTH & HELWYS

#Connect
Reaching Youth Across the Digital Divide
Brian Foreman

Reaching our youth across the digital divide is a struggle for parents, ministers, and other adults who work with Generation Z—today's teenagers. *#Connect* leads readers into the technological landscape, encourages conversations with teenagers, and reminds us all to be the presence of Christ in every facet of our lives.   978-1-57312-693-9   120 pages/pb   **$13.00**

Beginnings
A Reverend and a Rabbi Talk About the Stories of Genesis
Michael Smith and Rami Shapiro

Editor Aaron Herschel Shapiro declares that stories "must be retold—not just repeated, but reinvented, reimagined, and reexperienced" to remain vital in the world. Mike and Rami continue their conversations from the *Mount and Mountain* books, exploring the places where their traditions intersect and diverge, listening to each other as they respond to the stories of Genesis.   978-1-57312-772-1   202 pages/pb   **$18.00**

Choosing Gratitude
Learning to Love the Life You Have
James A. Autry

Autry reminds us that gratitude is a choice, a spiritual—not social—process. He suggests that if we cultivate gratitude as a way of being, we may not change the world and its ills, but we can change our response to the world. If we fill our lives with moments of gratitude, we will indeed love the life we have.   978-1-57312-614-4   144 pages/pb   **$15.00**

Choosing Gratitude 365 Days a Year
Your Daily Guide to Grateful Living
James A. Autry and Sally J. Pederson

Filled with quotes, poems, and the inspired voices of both Pederson and Autry, in a society consumed by fears of not having "enough"—money, possessions, security, and so on—this book suggests that if we cultivate gratitude as a way of being, we may not change the world and its ills, but we can change our response to the world.   978-1-57312-689-2   210 pages/pb   **$18.00**

To order call **1-800-747-3016** or visit **www.helwys.com**

Crisis Ministry: A Handbook
Daniel G. Bagby

Covering more than 25 crisis pastoral care situations, this book provides a brief, practical guide for church leaders and other caregivers responding to stressful situations in the lives of parishioners. It tells how to resource caregiving professionals in the community who can help people in distress.   978-1-57312-370-9   154 pages/pb   **$15.00**

Crossroads in Christian Growth
W. Loyd Allen

Authentic Christian life presents spiritual crises and we struggle to find a hero walking with God at a crossroads. With wisdom and sincerity, W. Loyd Allen presents Jesus as our example and these crises as stages in the journey of growth we each take toward maturity in Christ.   978-1-57312-753-0   164 pages/pb   **$15.00**

A Divine Duet
Ministry and Motherhood
Alicia Davis Porterfield, ed.

Each essay in this inspiring collection is as different as the mother-minister who wrote it, from theologians to chaplains, inner-city ministers to rural-poverty ministers, youth pastors to preachers, mothers who have adopted, birthed, and done both.   978-1-57312-676-2   146 pages/pb   **$16.00**

The Exile and Beyond (All the Bible series)
Wayne Ballard

The Exile and Beyond brings to life the sacred literature of Israel and Judah that comprises the exilic and postexilic communities of faith. It covers Ezekiel, Isaiah, Haggai, Zechariah, Malachi, 1 & 2 Chronicles, Ezra, Nehemiah, Joel, Jonah, Song of Songs, Esther, and Daniel.   978-1-57312-759-2   196 pages/pb   **$16.00**

Fierce Love
Desperate Measures for Desperate Times
Jeanie Miley

Fierce Love is about learning to see yourself and know yourself as a conduit of love, operating from a full heart instead of trying to find someone to whom you can hook up your emotional hose and fill up your empty heart.   978-1-57312-810-0   276 pages/pb   **$18.00**

To order call **1-800-747-3016** or visit **www.helwys.com**

Five Hundred Miles
Reflections on Calling and Pilgrimage
Lauren Brewer Bass

Spain's Camino de Santiago, the Way of St. James, has been a cherished pilgrimage path for centuries, visited by countless people searching for healing, solace, purpose, and hope. These stories from her five-hundred-mile-walk is Lauren Brewer Bass's honest look at the often winding, always surprising journey of a calling. *978-1-57312-812-4 142 pages/pb* **$16.00**

Galatians (Smyth & Helwys Bible Commentary)
Marion L. Soards and Darrell J. Pursiful

In Galatians, Paul endeavored to prevent the Gentile converts from embracing a version of the gospel that insisted on their observance of a form of the Mosaic Law. He saw with a unique clarity that such a message reduced the crucified Christ to being a mere agent of the Law. For Paul, the gospel of Jesus Christ alone, and him crucified, had no place in it for the claim that Law-observance was necessary for believers to experience the power of God's grace. *978-1-57312-771-4 384 pages/hc* **$55.00**

Glimpses from State Street
Wayne Ballard

As a collection of devotionals, Glimpses from State Street provides a wealth of insights and new ways to consider and develop our fellowship with Christ. It also serves as a window into the relationship between a small town pastor and a welcoming congregation.
978-1-57312-841-4 158 pages/pb **$15.00**

God's Servants, the Prophets
Bryan Bibb

God's Servants, the Prophets covers the Israelite and Judean prophetic literature from the preexilic period. It includes Amos, Hosea, Isaiah, Micah, Zephaniah, Nahum, Habakkuk, Jeremiah, and Obadiah.
978-1-57312-758-5 208 pages/pb **$16.00**

Gray Matters
100 Devotions for the Aging
Edwin Ray Frazier

"Each line rests on Frazier's fundamental belief that every season in life is valuable and rich with opportunity."

—Alicia Davis Porterfield
Interim pastor and former eldercare chaplain
978-1-57312-837-7 246 pages/pb **$18.00**

To order call **1-800-747-3016** or visit **www.helwys.com**

Hermeneutics of Hymnody
A Comprehensive and Integrated Approach to Understanding Hymns
Scotty Gray

Scotty Gray's *Hermeneutics of Hymnody* is a comprehensive and integrated approach to understanding hymns. It is unique in its holistic and interrelated exploration of seven of the broad facets of this most basic forms of Christian literature. A chapter is devoted to each and relates that facet to all of the others. 978-157312-767-7 *432 pages/pb* **$28.00**

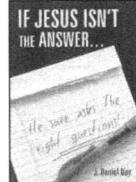

If Jesus Isn't the Answer . . . He Sure Asks the Right Questions!
J. Daniel Day

Taking eleven of Jesus' questions as its core, Day invites readers into their own conversation with Jesus. Equal parts testimony, theological instruction, pastoral counseling, and autobiography, the book is ultimately an invitation to honest Christian discipleship.
978-1-57312-797-4 *148 pages/pb* **$16.00**

I'm Trying to Lead . . . Is Anybody Following?
The Challenge of Congregational Leadership in the Postmodern World
Charles B. Bugg

Bugg provides us with a view of leadership that has theological integrity, honors the diversity of church members, and reinforces the brave hearts of church leaders who offer vision and take risks in the service of Christ and the church. 978-1-57312-731-8 *136 pages/pb* **$13.00**

James M. Dunn and Soul Freedom
Aaron Douglas Weaver

James Milton Dunn, over the last fifty years, has been the most aggressive Baptist proponent for religious liberty in the US. Soul freedom—voluntary, uncoerced faith and an unfettered individual conscience before God—is the basis of his understanding of church-state separation and the historic Baptist basis of religious liberty.
978-1-57312-590-1 *224 pages/pb* **$18.00**

Judaism
A Brief Guide to Faith and Practice
Sharon Pace

Sharon Pace's newest book is a sensitive and comprehensive introduction to Judaism. How does belief in the One God and a universal morality shape the way in which Jews see the world? How does one find meaning in life and the courage to endure suffering? How does one mark joy and forge community ties? 978-1-57312-644-1 *144 pages/pb* **$16.00**

To order call 1-800-747-3016 or visit www.helwys.com

Luke (Smyth & Helwys Annual Bible Study series)
Parables for the Journey
Michael L. Ruffin

These stories in Luke's Gospel are pilgrimage parables. They are parables for those on the way to being the people of God. They are not places where we stop and stay; they are rather places where we learn what we need to learn and from which, equipped with Jesus' directions, we continue the journey. But we will see that they are also places to which we repeatedly return.

Teaching Guide 978-1-57312-849-0 146 pages/pb **$14.00**
Study Guide 978-1-57312-850-6 108 pages/pb **$6.00**

Meditations on Mark
Daily Devotions from the Oldest Gospel
Chris Cadenhead

Readers searching for a fresh encounter with Scripture can delve into *Meditations on Mark*, a collection of daily devotions intended to guide the reader through the book of Mark, the Oldest Gospel and the first known effort to summarize and proclaim the life and ministry of Jesus.

978-1-57312-851-3 158 pages/pb **$15.00**

Meeting Jesus Today
For the Cautious, the Curious, and the Committed
Jeanie Miley

Meeting Jesus Today, ideal for both individual study and small groups, is intended to be used as a workbook. It is designed to move readers from studying the Scriptures and ideas within the chapters to recording their journey with the Living Christ.

978-1-57312-677-9 320 pages/pb **$19.00**

The Ministry Life
101 Tips for New Ministers
John Killinger

Sharing years of wisdom from more than fifty years in ministry and teaching, *The Ministry Life: 101 Tips for New Ministers* by John Killinger is filled with practical advice and wisdom for a minister's day-to-day tasks as well as advice on intellectual and spiritual habits to keep ministers of any age healthy and fulfilled.

978-1-57312-662-5 244 pages/pb **$19.00**

To order call **1-800-747-3016** or visit **www.helwys.com**

Mount and Mountain
Vol. 2: A Reverend and a Rabbi Talk About the Sermon on the Mount
Rami Shapiro and Michael Smith

This book, focused on the Sermon on the Mount, represents the second half of Mike and Rami's dialogue. In it, Mike and Rami explore the text of Jesus' sermon cooperatively, contributing perspectives drawn from their lives and religious traditions and seeking moments of illumination.

978-1-57312-654-0 254 pages/pb **$19.00**

Of Mice and Ministers
Musings and Conversations About Life, Death, Grace, and Everything
Bert Montgomery

With stories about pains, joys, and everyday life, *Of Mice and Ministers* finds Jesus in some unlikely places and challenges us to do the same. From tattooed women ministers to saying the "N"-word to the brotherly kiss, Bert Montgomery takes seriously the lesson from Psalm 139—where can one go that God is not already there?

978-1-57312-733-2 154 pages/pb **$14.00**

Place Value
The Journey to Where You Are
Katie Sciba

Does a place have value? Can a place change us? Is it possible for God to use the place you are in to form you? From Victoria, Texas to Indonesia, Belize, Australia, and beyond, Katie Sciba's wanderlust serves as a framework to understand your own places of deep emotion and how God may have been weaving redemption around you all along.

978-157312-829-2 138 pages/pb **$15.00**

Reading Joshua
(Reading the Old Testament series)
A Historical-Critical/Archaeological Commentary
John C. H. Laughlin

Using the best of current historical-critical studies by mainstream biblical scholars, and the most recent archaeological discoveries and theorizing, Laughlin questions both the historicity of the stories presented in the book as well as the basic theological ideology presented through these stories: namely that Yahweh ordered the indiscriminate butchery of the Canaanites.

978-1-57312-836-0 274 pages/pb **$32.00**

To order call **1-800-747-3016** or visit **www.helwys.com**

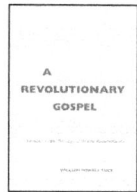

A Revolutionary Gospel
Salvation in the Theology of Walter Rauschenbusch
William Powell Tuck

William Powell Tuck describes how Rauschenbusch's concept of redemption requires a transformation of society as well as individuals—and that no one can genuinely be redeemed without this redemption affecting the social culture as well. *A Revolutionary Gospel* shows us how Rauschenbusch's revolutionary concept of salvation is still relevant today.

978-1-57312-804-9 190 pages/pb **$21.00**

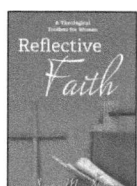

Reflective Faith
A Theological Toolbox for Women
Susan M. Shaw

In *Reflective Faith*, Susan Shaw offers a set of tools to explore difficult issues of biblical interpretation, theology, church history, and ethics—especially as they relate to women. Reflective faith invites intellectual struggle and embraces the unknown; it is a way of discipleship, a way to love God with your mind, as well as your heart, your soul, and your strength.

978-1-57312-719-6 292 pages/pb **$24.00**
Workbook 978-1-57312-754-7 164 pages/pb **$12.00**

Sessions with Ephesians (Sessions Bible Studies series)
Toward a New Identity in Christ
William L. Self & Michael D. McCullar

Ephesians has been called "the most contemporary book in the Bible." Strip it of just a few first-century references and it would be easily applicable to the modern church.

978-1-57312-838-4 110 pages/pb **$14.00**

Sessions with Psalms (Sessions Bible Studies series)
Prayers for All Seasons
Eric and Alicia D. Porterfield

Useful to seminar leaders during preparation and group discussion, as well as in individual Bible study, *Sessions with Psalms* is a ten-session study designed to explore what it looks like for the words of the psalms to become the words of our prayers. Each session is followed by a thought-provoking page of questions.

978-1-57312-768-4 136 pages/pb **$14.00**

To order call **1-800-747-3016** or visit **www.helwys.com**

Tell the Truth, Shame the Devil
Stories about the Challenges of Young Pastors
James Elllis III, ed.

A pastor's life is uniquely difficult. *Tell the Truth, Shame the Devil*, then, is an attempt to expose some of the challenges that young clergy often face. While not exhaustive, this collection of essays is a superbly compelling and diverse introduction to how tough being a pastor under the age of thirty-five can be.   978-1-57312-839-1 198 pages/pb **$18.00**

Though the Darkness Gather Round
Devotions about Infertility, Miscarriage, and Infant Loss
Mary Elizabeth Hill Hanchey and Erin McClain, eds.

Much courage is required to weather the long grief of infertility and the sudden grief of miscarriage and infant loss. This collection of devotions by men and women, ministers, chaplains, and lay leaders who can speak of such sorrow, is a much-needed resource and precious gift for families on this journey and the faith communities that walk beside them.

    978-1-57312-811-7 180 pages/pb **$19.00**

Time for Supper
Invitations to Christ's Table
Brett Younger

Some scholars suggest that every meal in literature is a communion scene. Could every meal in the Bible be a communion text? Could every passage be an invitation to God's grace? These meditations on the Lord's Supper help us listen to the myriad of ways God invites us to gratefully, reverently, and joyfully share the cup of Christ.   978-1-57312-720-2 246 pages/pb **$18.00**

A Time to Laugh
Humor in the Bible
Mark E. Biddle

With characteristic liveliness, Mark E. Biddle explores the ways humor was intentionally incorporated into Scripture. Drawing on Biddle's command of Hebrew language and cultural subtleties, *A Time to Laugh* guides the reader through the stories of six biblical characters who did rather unexpected things.   978-1-57312-683-0 164 pages/pb **$14.00**

To order call **1-800-747-3016** or visit **www.helwys.com**

A True Hope
Jedi Perils and the Way of Jesus
Joshua Hays

Star Wars offers an accessible starting point for considering substantive issues of faith, philosophy, and ethics. In *A True Hope*, Joshua Hays explores some of these challenging ideas through the sayings of the Jedi Masters, examining the ways the worldview of the Jedi is at odds with that of the Bible. 978-1-57312-770-7 *186 pages/pb* **$18.00**

Word of God Across the Ages
Using Christian History in Preaching
Bill J. Leonard

In this third, enlarged edition, Bill J. Leonard returns to the roots of the Christian story to find in the lives of our faithful forebears examples of the potent presence of the gospel. Through these stories, those who preach today will be challenged and inspired as they pursue the divine Word in human history through the ages. 978-1-57312-828-5 *174 pages/pb* **$19.00**

The World Is Waiting for You
Celebrating the 50th Ordination Anniversary of Addie Davis
Pamela R. Durso & LeAnn Gunter Johns, eds.

Hope for the church and the world is alive and well in the words of these gifted women. Keen insight, delightful observations, profound courage, and a gift for communicating the good news are woven throughout these sermons. The Spirit so evident in Addie's calling clearly continues in her legacy. 978-1-57312-732-5 *224 pages/pb* **$18.00**

With Us in the Wilderness
Finding God's Story in Our Lives
Laura A. Barclay

What stories compose your spiritual biography? In *With Us in the Wilderness*, Laura Barclay shares her own stories of the intersection of the divine and the everyday, guiding readers toward identifying and embracing God's presence in their own narratives.
978-1-57312-721-9 *120 pages/pb* **$13.00**

To order call **1-800-747-3016** or visit **www.helwys.com**

Clarence Jordan's
Cotton Patch Gospel

The Complete Collection

Hardback • 448 pages
Retail ~~50.00~~ • Your Price 25.00

Paperback • 448 pages
Retail ~~40.00~~ • Your Price 20.00

The Cotton Patch Gospel, by Koinonia Farm founder Clarence Jordan, recasts the stories of Jesus and the letters of the New Testament into the language and culture of the mid-twentieth-century South. Born out of the civil rights struggle, these now-classic translations of much of the New Testament bring the far-away places of Scripture closer to home: Gainesville, Selma, Birmingham, Atlanta, Washington D.C.

More than a translation, *The Cotton Patch Gospel* continues to make clear the startling relevance of Scripture for today. Now for the first time collected in a single, hardcover volume, this edition comes complete with a new Introduction by President Jimmy Carter, a Foreword by Will D. Campbell, and an Afterword by Tony Campolo. Smyth & Helwys Publishing is proud to help reintroduce these seminal works of Clarence Jordan to a new generation of believers, in an edition that can be passed down to generations still to come.

To order call **1-800-747-3016**
or visit **www.helwys.com**

www.ingramcontent.com/pod-product-compliance
Lightning Source LLC
Chambersburg PA
CBHW070541090426
42735CB00013B/3039